EASYMADE
AND
COUNTRY DRINKS

Mrs. Gennery-Taylor

RIGHT WAY

Printed and bound in Great Britain by Cox & Wyman Ltd., Reading, Berkshire.

The *Right Way* series and the *Paperfronts* series are both published by Elliot Right Way Books, Brighton Road, Lower Kingswood, Tadworth, Surrey, KT20 6TD, U.K.

PREFACE

I hope this book will be helpful to those who wish to make a few bottles for home consumption or for giving to friends.

I have tried to show that good wine can be made in small quantities and with simple equipment. All the fruits, vegetables and flowers in the recipes are ones it should be easy to gather from field or hedgerow, or which can be obtained in dried form. I therefore hope my book will encourage some of you to start this fascinating hobby with the added pleasure of harvesting most of your own ingredients.

I should also like to thank those friends who have so kindly let me use their own special recipes.

Do remember that although you can give your wines to your friends, the law forbids you sell it!

PUBLISHER'S NOTE

The Publishers wish to acknowledge their gratitude for the vast range of help given by Derek Pearman formerly of W. R. Loftus Ltd., London, specialist suppliers of home wine-making equipment and sundries over several generations. In re-shaping the country wine recipes in this book he has, in the main, introduced inexpensive modern equipment and products only on the grounds of saving effort and time for today's enthusiast. However, to preserve the identity of Mrs. Gennery-Taylor's great original book a number of recipes have been left as they stood or only altered in a minor way. For example, in Bullace Plum Wine, Damson (first method), Rhubarb (second method) and Sloe Wine the method of allowing mould to form has been retained.

In the recipe for Hip Wine, the original recipe relying on wild yeast only, has been given. It takes a little longer for the wine to be made but it is arguable that a more genuine and finer taste results. Readers who wish to experiment and follow her early "country" wild yeast method may choose to adapt recipes for some of the other wines such as: Apple, Damson, Gooseberry, Grape, Greengage, Lemon, Loganberry, Redcurrant, Rhubarb, Strawberry, Tomato and compare results of the time-honoured way with the quality of wines they can make nowadays, using speedier techniques.

DEDICATION

I affectionately dedicate this book to my parents and to Charles for suggesting it, I say, 'thank you'.

CONTENTS

PART I: GENERAL INSTRUCTIONS

PART II: WINES

PART III: WINE RECIPES

PART IV: OTHER DRINKS

PART V: CHILDREN'S DRINKS, TEAS AND COFFEES

PART I
GENERAL INSTRUCTIONS

EARLY DAYS

Soon after I married I decided to make some wine. I had never made any and had no idea how to begin. I remembered that my grandmother used to make excellent wine, but I was a child then – too young to learn.

I was lucky, however, in having a good friend who could make wine. To her it was an inherited accomplishment, handed down from one generation to another, as necessary to housekeeping and cooking.

She gave me a recipe for rhubarb wine and as it was springtime there was plenty of rhubarb about. I followed her directions carefully and found everything absurdly simple. But still I didn't believe that this fruit juice could become wine.

I filled the wine bottles and placed them in a cool dark cupboard. Never was a wine watched so carefully. I inspected and tasted it nearly every day. Hapless visitors were forced to try it, but my husband revolted – he would rather wait till it was ready to drink.

Somehow I managed to save two bottles for six months and found, secretly to my surprise, that it had turned into a very pleasant wine. This greatly encouraged me, and I began to make different kinds and have done so ever since.

Of course I had some failures; sometimes I was careless and the winefly got in and turned the wine sour.

Other times I left too much airspace above the wine when I finally bottled it and this caused the wine to turn sharp. But gradually I learned to be careful and watch for these things.

Although we are not constantly drinking wine, I rarely

seem to keep a bottle for much more than a year to mature properly. I firmly hide several bottles, but there is always that special occasion which seems to demand a bottle of wine. So my stock dwindles.

I love trying new recipes or inventing my own.

I FIND THAT THE MAIN VIRTUE NEEDED FOR WINEMAKING IS PATIENCE.

ECONOMY

One thing that consoles me when I see my wine disappearing so quickly is that it is much cheaper than shop wine.

I believe that home-made wine can cost less than a tenth of the price of the cheapest shop wine. In many cases, where wild fruits or flowers are gathered, sugar is the only major ingredient to be bought. So this wine costs no more than a few pence a bottle.

One can also be extravagant in using it for cooking. Home-made wines can often take the place of white wine or sherry. There is no need to use the wine sparingly when one knows there are some more bottles in the cellar.

UTENSILS AND CONTAINERS

Please do not be put off making wine by the thought of the expensive equipment to be bought. Most of us have a large saucepan or preserving pan which will do to boil those ingredients which need boiling.

METAL CONTAINERS MAY BE USED AT THIS STAGE, *BUT MUST NEVER BE USED TO HOLD FERMENTING WINE* (EXCEPT STAINLESS STEEL).

Next you need a large bowl, a big earthenware mixing bowl will do. A plastic bucket makes an excellent container for your mix, because it is light, easily cleaned and easy to cover. To have two buckets is a great advantage.

Certain coloured buckets are thought to be unsuitable due to their method of manufacture and it is wise to check that your buckets are recommended for food use.

Bottles are the next item. Keep all your old wine bottles,

those that were corked are the best.

The things you will need are:

1 large saucepan or preserving pan.

2 large earthenware bowls or plastic buckets.

A plastic spoon.

A piece of muslin or a straining bag.

A plastic funnel.

2 x 1 gallon demi-johns

A supply of demi-john corks if you are storing in the demi-john (see below).

Airlock

Bored rubber demi-john bungs to fit airlock with.

Clear flexible plastic siphon tube – a metre long

Thermometer

Wine hydrometer (optional but recommended)

Hydrometer jar (optional)

Wine bottles and corks

Corking machine

If you wish to make sufficient wine to be able to enjoy it freely and to build up a mature stock for special occasions, it is advisable to make not less than a gallon at a time. Two or three gallons can be made with little extra effort other than having the extra equipment to hand and multiplying the quantities of ingredients. For those who want to make larger quantities, five gallon units could be used, along with a five gallon plastic or glass container.

Earthenware crocks, formerly used, are becoming scarce; they are comparatively expensive, heavy and harder to handle. Wooden casks are favoured by advanced amateur winemakers fortunate enough to possess them, but they require careful use and are certainly not essential, as good wine can be made with the simple equipment specified in this book.

For storage after the wine is made you may find that demi-johns are more appropriate to the way you will drink the wine than individual bottles. If the whole demi-john is likely to be drunk within a week it can simply be drawn off a decanter at a time. A cork-bung is preferable to rubber for storing in a demi-john to avoid risk of tainting the wine over a period.

All the equipment described should be easily obtainable from your local wine-making equipment shop or specialist department of a multiple store, chemist, etc.

These shops specialise in the supply of home-made wine equipment and a visit to their premises or a request for their catalogue is an education.

STERILIZATION

It is important that all utensils and bottles used in making and storing wine should be thoroughly sterilized, both before and after use. Washing with boiling water is not good enough. Obtain from your specialist shop or chemist, a supply of sodium meta-bisulphite and use in the proportions instructed on the container. In the absence of specific instructions $\frac{1}{2}$oz. of sodium meta-bisulphite per quart of water should be sufficient. Once dissolved in the water this solution can be kept in a suitable screw-top bottle and can be used repeatedly to sterilize all equipment provided the bottle is kept closed after use. Wash your equipment first, then rinse with the sodium meta-bisulphite solution for sterilization. WARNING: Inhaling the fumes from the solution should be avoided.

Corks also need to be sterilized and the best approach is to soak them in hot water (do not boil) to which has been added a campden tablet. If you soak for about $\frac{1}{2}$ an hour, just before you are ready to use them, the corks will then be slightly softened making them easier to drive into the bottles.

STRAINING THE WINE

I find muslin the best material for straining wines. Straining is most easily done by laying the muslin across a plastic flour sifter (borrowed from kitchen); lodging the sifter across a plastic bucket and pouring the wine through.

On no account use a metal strainer as this could react to the acid in the wine.

Specialist retailers can supply straining bags which may be preferred as they can easily be washed and re-used. Whether a fresh bag or an old one is being used it should always be sterilised before and after use. Squeeze the last drops through when straining but not to the extent that any pulp passes through.

YEASTS

The yeast I have suggested in the recipes is general purpose (G.P.) wine yeast, sometimes described as A.P. or all purpose yeast. G.P. yeast is considered far superior to the old-fashioned bakers' or brewers' yeasts which used to be mentioned in early wine recipes. (The exception is beer for which you must obtain brewers' yeast.) All yeasts sold for wine-making carry descriptive labelling indicating the correct amount to use per unit of volume of liquid.

For those who can afford it selected wine yeasts can provide further refinement. These can be obtained in dry or liquid form on the advice of your specialist supplier. Used appropriately they not only maximise bouquet and alcoholic degree, usually the clarifying of the resultant wine is also much easier. These cultured yeasts are always sold with full instructions which should be adhered to strictly.

For the yeast to carry out its work energetically it is a great advantage for it to have additional nourishment rather like humans need extra food if they are engaged in a lot of physical activity. For this reason yeast nutrient is added to all the recipes. The quantity required must be determined by careful reference to the instructions given by the supplier.

When making large quantities of wine such as five or ten gallons it is advisable to activate the yeast before hand to build up the colony prior to adding it to your ingredients. This is usually referred to as making a "starter". The following instructions may differ slightly from those you read on packets, etc., but you will find them quite adequate. Remember to prepare your yeast starter in advance.

11

Specially designed starter bottles can be obtained from your wine making equipment supplier and may be preferred. They have a built-in diaphragm in the cap to control the pressure and are manufactured in plastic.

To prepare the starter take a large tonic water bottle and sterilize it. Boil sufficient water to half fill the bottle and add to this the juice of an orange, and then half a teaspoonful of sugar plus your yeast nutrient. Allow this mixture to cool to below 70°F (20°C). Drop your yeast into the sterilized bottle (if it is in tablet form crush first) and pour in the cooled prepared mixture. Thoroughly shake and then plug the neck lightly with cotton wool. Store in a warm temperature of 70°F — 75°F (20°C - 24°C), shaking occasionally. After five or six hours activity should be apparent and the starter is ready to use. The full activity of the yeast can only commence when it is introduced into the must, its natural living medium. The prior cultivation of the yeast in this way helps to make sure that it can disperse and work throughout a larger quantity of wine more easily. A starter made from specialized cultured yeast may need several days before it becomes active, read instructions supplied with it carefully.

FERMENTATION

Throughout this book, sugar is an ingredient in every recipe. In countries where sugar may be scarce, glucose (wheat sugar) has the same fermentation qualities as granulated sugar and can be used instead. It should be used weight for weight (1 lb. of glucose for 1 lb. of sugar).

Fermentation begins in the plastic bucket, after sugar and yeast have been added and it has been covered with a clean linen cloth secured with elastic or string. It requires some warmth and an air space below the covering material; therefore at this stage keep the container in a place where the ROOM temperature is maintained just around or above 70°F (20°C). If the container is nearly full some liquid will froth over.

One can tell if wine is fermenting by listening, as a faint hissing noise will be heard.

Fermentation in the plastic bucket should be continued generally for five – seven days for soft fruits and seven – ten days for hard fruits, after which the liquid is strained into a fermentation demi-john. These are minimum periods and a little more time can be allowed safely and profitably provided that the plastic bucket is covered effectively.

THE WINEFLY

Wines fermenting in bowls or other containers must always be covered closely with a clean cloth to prevent the winefly from entering. This tiny fly appears almost from nowhere, it seems, at the mere whiff of fermenting wine. If it does get into the wine in large numbers it will soon turn it sour, so be most careful to keep the bowl completely covered.

USING THE FERMENTATION DEMI-JOHN

The strained wine is transferred into a sterile fermentation demi-john by using a sterile plastic funnel. If the wine is fermenting vigorously, do not fill to the top of the demi-john as it might froth over. Fit an airlock to prevent the air from getting in. When the fermentation has subsided somewhat, complete the filling of the demi-john to within one inch of the base of the bung and allow the fermenting wine to continue until the fermentation has stopped. A further period is then allowed for the wine to clear – see also under the heading Clearing the Wine. The whole process during which the fermenting continues to dryness (maximum alcoholic content) and the wine clears itself thereafter, can take two – three months depending on the type of wine being made.

There are many types of fermentation lock available. They have taken the place of the old-fashioned method of covering jars, etc., with cloth or muslin, which only kept out the dust but did not exclude the airborne bacteria which so often infected the wine and ultimately turned it to vinegar.

Airlocks can be used with any type of vessel providing you have the right size bored cork or bung to fit the neck. The most popular type of air-lock used is the one which has bulbs on either side of a 'U' bend. The 'U' portion only is first filled with water which has been sterilized with a campden tablet or sodium meta-bisulphite as an added safeguard. During fermentation the water in the airlock is pushed to one side as the gases bubble through to the atmosphere. When fermentation ceases, the water will fall back level in the 'U' portion of the lock, indicating the end of fermentation. Care should be taken when fitting airlocks to ensure that the corks or bungs are sterilized and of good quality to form a good seal. Otherwise the gases will escape through the cork and not pass through the lock and airborne bacteria may find their way in. Rubber bungs are recommended as they form a better seal and are easier to sterilize. Fitting the lock to the bung is easiest while it is still wet from sterilizing. The bottom end of the lock must not project too far down. On no account must it touch the wine otherwise the object of using it will be defeated and the bung will blow out as the pressure builds up. Extracting an airlock from the ceiling can be quite tricky! Once the lock is secure no contamination from the atmosphere can affect the wine.

Judging when the fermentation has stopped can be done by:

1) Noting that no bubbles at all are now passing through the airlock and the liquid in the 'U' bend has returned to level.

2) Adding a tablespoonful of sugar to the wine. If it fizzes and bubbles up it is still working and a little more sugar should be added until fermentation is complete. If no reaction, fermentation has now finished.

3) Using a hydrometer to tell the specific gravity of the wine which will tell you if all the sugar has been used up. Normally a reading of 1.000 or just below means that the wine has fermented to dryness.

The hydrometer is sold with full instructions and can also be used to establish the percentage alcohol content if so desired.

Adding sugar in small quantities to complete the

fermentation as described above is known as feeding the wine. To allow space for the extra sugar it may be necessary to siphon the wine off the deposit so far formed, into another demi-john, or even lose a little wine.

Remember that yeasts are living organisms that you employ to convert your sweetened juice into an alcoholic beverage. Providing they are kept warm and given the right balance of sugar and nutrient to encourage them to work no problems will arise.

The amount of sugar in the recipes has been carefully calculated and only a few may need extra feeding. When you do feed on no account saturate the juice with excess sugar, otherwise the yeast will 'go on strike' and you may end up with a wine so sweet as to be undrinkable.

While most people know that yeast converts sugar into alcohol, many do not appreciate that it is wrong to therefore assume that the more sugar added the more alcohol will be produced. In reality when we introduce a yeast to a sweetened juice it begins to dig its own grave. When it has dug deep enough, or reached its alcoholic tolerance, it comes to rest. Sad, you might say, but treat it with respect while it is living and it will produce good wine for you.

Wine connoisseurs may like to take note that the recipes contained in this book *are* country wines and for that reason tend towards being sweet wines. If you desire your wine to have a drier taste, you can reduce the amount of sugar in any of the wine recipes to accord with your personal taste. However, you should never reduce the amount below 2 lb. of sugar.

Occasionally you may find a wine is not sweet enough for your personal taste and in this case it can be sweetened before drinking using a non-fermentable sweetener which is easily obtained from specialist shops.

RACKING

When fermentation is finished, it is time to put the wine into a second sterile demi-john into which is first crushed a campden tablet. It is a simple operation to syphon off the wine with a thin plastic tube without disturbing the sediment or lees, which will be visible at the bottom, into the second demi-john. This process is known as racking.

The demi-john must be securely corked with a safety cork which has a non-return valve to keep the air out. Alternatively you can use the airlock and rubber bung again. The point is, keep the air out.

If it is not already clear the wine should begin to clear itself. Some wines take much longer than others to clear and here patience will be essential. It is very important to be sure that the fermentation has finished before you rack. Occasionally a second racking and even a third can be an advantage in obtaining a really clear wine. This would be indicated where a substantial amount of sediment has built up at the bottom without the wine becoming clear and is a matter of judgement and experience. There is also a danger, should the wine sit on its sediment too long, of the decomposing matter affecting the flavour.

CLEARING THE WINE

Wines should clear themselves in time, and even a stubborn wine will clear eventually. However, if you wish to hasten the process, a suitable clearing agent can be added 3-4 weeks after the first racking. These are readily available from specialist shops. The most common ones are finings and bentonite for general use — amylase for clearing starch haze (grain based recipes) – and pectin destroying enzyme for fruit or vegetable wines.

A pectin destroying enzyme will normally only be required in a fruit or vegetable wine where the recipe has included hot water poured over or boiling the ingredients. It is the heat that brings the pectin out of the fruit or vegetable, causing the trouble. In the case of a pectin destroying enzyme it is an advantage for it to be added earlier and it is normally put in at the same time as the campden tablet and the yeast, or 24 hours earlier than the yeast should this be instructed on the package.

16

STORING WINE

Ideally, wine should be stored in a cool dark place, preferably on a stone floor, at a temperature of 55° Fahrenheit (13°C). But it survives quite well under less perfect conditions. So don't worry if you live in a flat with no nice cool cellar or pantry. Find a cupboard that is not too near a fireplace, and use that.

It is best to inspect the bottles fairly often as the corks do sometimes pop out, then the little winefly pops in and turns the wine sour.

It has been suggested that the wine bottles should be turned on their sides as professional wine-makers do. This might, however, be difficult in the home where storage space is often limited, or if there is any doubt about how tightly the corks are fitted. I think if the bottles are filled and the corks pushed in tightly this should prevent the corks from drying out and shrinking and so letting in the air. As a precaution, the tops of the corks may be waxed.

Although proper wine corks can be pushed in if they have been soaked for 30 – 40 minutes as described under sterilizing, it is by no means always easy to drive them fully home. Several simple corking machines are available and can quickly repay their investment.

Whether you are storing the wine in bottles or going to keep it in demi-johns to save space, these must always be washed and sterilized before use. It is important that the receptacle is filled to approximately 1 inch from the bottom of the cork or bung. Excessive air space above the wine may otherwise risk bacterial contamination.

Bottling is carried out in the same way as racking using a plastic tube to siphon the liquid. It is usual to rack into a sterile demi-john as a final stage before bottling in order to make sure only clear wine reaches the bottles.

CAMPDEN TABLETS

The purpose of campden tablets is to protect the must from infection and from oxidisation. The tablets are usually crushed into the liquid and they work by giving off sulphur dioxide (SO_2) which, being heavier than air, forms a 'blanket' which remains over the liquid giving the protection. It is often recommended that the yeast is not added until 24 hours after the campden tablet and this is because initially its action may inhibit fermentation.

When the yeast goes in and begins working it forms its own protective layer of carbon dioxide (CO_2) in a similar fashion and takes over the protective function itself. An additional campden tablet is recommended at the first racking for continuing protection during the period in which the wine clears and to prevent the possibility of oxidisation. Further protection is rarely necessary although another campden tablet may be added for peace of mind at each racking.

BASIC AMOUNTS AND METHODS

PREPARATION

Fruit or vegetables are generally washed, then cut up or sliced to increase their surface area. Avoid cutting pips or seeds in half, remove stones and always remove pith or your wine will turn out having a very bitter taste. Some people warn you to look out for maggots – others are not sure they don't improve the flavour!

Flowers need to be washed to remove any insects, etc., and it is usual to remove the stalks. In the flower recipes it helps during the initial fermentation in the plastic bucket if, when stirring each day, the flowers are squeezed against the side to extract the maximum amount of goodness. This is called 'maceration'.

Where recipes include raisin juice prepare in advance as follows: Place them in a suitable plastic or earthenware bowl and cover with boiling water. Leave them for 24 hours to swell and absorb the water. Then press out the juice using a masher or empty milk bottle and strain it ready for use.

AMOUNTS

You may find you wish to make wine from some non-poisonous fruit, flower or vegetable not mentioned in this book. Although you may notice a few recipes in this book use cold water only, it is usually the case that a hot water method will be more likely to work well. The general rules are:

For tough-skinned fruits and roots: These will need boiling and perhaps simmering initially in a preserving pan or large saucepan until the ingredients become tender. For flowers and soft fruits no boiling is required. Instead you simply pour boiling water over the fruit or flowers.

To allow for evaporation, recipes where boiling and simmering is appropriate generally need one gallon of water at the start (plus the ingredients) in order to yield one gallon of wine. Recipes where you are pouring boiling water over the fruit, flowers or vegetables only need six pints of water per one gallon of wine.

Use three – four pounds of fruit or vegetable matter, or three quarts – a gallon of flowers (pushed down but remaining springy) and $2\frac{1}{2}$ lb of sugar. Add juice and the chopped peel (not the pith) of one orange and one lemon to vegetable and flower recipes. Vegetable and grain recipes also need prepared juice from $\frac{1}{2}$ lb. raisins as described above, while flower and grain recipes are much improved with the addition of tannin in order to create a well balanced must. The tannin although not essential puts life and zest into what could otherwise be described as a wine lacking character. Its presence also helps with clearing and maturing. Tannin can be purchased in powder or liquid form from your specialist shop and half a teaspoonful will be sufficient in such recipes. Alternatively use half a cupful of cold strong tea.

You can experiment a little, but if you follow these main quantities you can't go far wrong. Halving the ingredients to make less wine will not affect its strength.

N.B. *Metric measures:* Since measures are always a little approximate you will find it sufficient to treat 1 gallon as $4\frac{1}{2}$ litres, and 2 lb. as 1 kilo.

Most of us appreciate a fine bouquet. When they are in season, try adding two heads of elderflower to your recipes, fermenting them with the other ingredients. The improved bouquet may even be associated with that of a Hock or a Moselle! Gooseberry First Method includes this suggestion.

METHOD

Make sure all your equipment is properly sterilized, see page 10.

We will start from where you have done the boiling and simmering, if it is a fruit or vegetable which requires to be made tender, and then transferred the mixture to your sterile plastic bucket or, in the case of ingredients which do not need this treatment, you are ready with the ingredients in the sterile plastic bucket and can begin by pouring the boiling water over them. The steps are then as follows:

1. Add sugar and stir well to dissolve. At this stage add such items as juice and chopped peel of lemon and orange, prepared raisin juice and/or tannin as called for by the particular recipe.

2. Allow mixture to cool, securely covered with clean linen cloth.

3. When the temperature of the mixture is down to 75°F (24°C), add one crushed campden tablet. In a fruit or vegetable wine also add a pectin destroying enzyme. Re-cover.

4. Some manufacturers of the above additives recommend you to leave the mixture for 24 hours before adding yeast. If so put the bucket in a warm place where the ROOM temperature is maintained just around or above 70°F (20°C).

5. Add GP or AP (general or all purpose) yeast and yeast nutrient in the quantities recommended by their manufacturers and cover again.

6. Leave the mixture to ferment in the bucket in a place where ROOM temperature is maintained at or just above 70°F (20°C) for 5 – 7 days with soft ingredients or 7 – 10 days for tougher ones. During this period the mixture should be stirred well daily and re-covered. The position must be warm for the yeast to work.

7. Strain through a sterile straining bag or muslin into a sterile demi-john.

8. Fit a sterile airlock.

9. Fermentation now continues and you leave the liquid until fermentation is complete, again in a ROOM temperature at or just above 70°F (20°C). This may take three to four weeks (or sometimes a lot longer!). Fermentation is complete when the solution or water levels in your airlock equalise, or no more bubbles are seen passing through it, no matter how slowly. The wine may also have started to look brighter and clearer.

10. Rack into a second sterile demi-john into which a campden tablet has been crushed. At this stage if any topping up is required – and the demi-john should be full to the bottom of the neck – do it with cold boiled water.

11. The wine should now be moved to a cool dark place, ideally on a stone floor, where the ROOM temperature remains around 55°F (13°C).

12. You now wait for the wine to clear and this normally takes several weeks. However, if the wine has not cleared after three or four weeks and you wish to hasten the process, you can add a suitable clearing agent, for which refer to page 16. As a general rule a wine will clear itself eventually.

Should a substantial amount of sediment accumulate during the clearing you are recommended to re-rack in the same way as before. It is not unusual to have to rack some wines two or three times during the clearing process.

13. Once the wine has cleared you may choose to store in the demi-john, bottling it just a day or two before you wish to drink it, or bottle it immediately if you prefer (see storage, page 17). One advantage of storage in the demi-john is that any sedimentation which happens to occur during the period of maturation never reaches the bottles.

14. Maturation periods vary but six months would be a usual minimum and a wine which is not ready to drink after a year may prove to be one of those unlucky failures. Of course, you may keep it longer and most wines go on improving, although we would not advise laying every

variety down for your children!

In many recipes I have mentioned a time when I consider the wine at its best for drinking. However, this is based on personal experience and taste and may deter the impatient!

Once fermentation is complete you have a finished wine although it is usually somewhat cloudy and unmatured. Few would want to taste it until it has cleared and its appearance has become acceptable but there is nothing to stop you trying it once this has happened and if the taste then appeals to you, carrying on and enjoying it. In case you wonder whether drinking it early means you are missing a better matured wine you can always label a few bottles and keep them over longer periods before drinking.

I have not set the amount of GP wine yeast, yeast nutrient or pectin destroying enzyme to use because, depending where you have bought them, they may have different working strengths per amount. However, the right quantity is always stated on the packet or tub, etc., and the manufacturers' instructions can be reliably followed.

KEEPING RECORDS

Keeping a record book enables you to see at any time what stage each making has reached and, especially if you are making several varieties simultaneously, ensures nothing gets forgotten. If you experiment here and there it is jolly annoying the next time, when you cannot remember what it was you did to make a particular batch of wine into an outstanding one! My notes follow a basic plan with room for any remarks which crop up!

Name of Wine: _____

Date begun: . . .   Ready to drink: . . .

Date bottled: . . .   Number of bottles recipe

Batch number:* . . .   produced: . . .

* If you are making several wines at once careful labelling at all stages is essential. Use of a batch number makes it easy to chalk quickly on to demi-johns and bottles.

Recipe

(I jot down where the recipe came from, e.g. Easymade Wine, page XX. With recipes passed on by friends or relations, I always write out in full detail rather than have to trust to memory a year later!)

Working tick-list (√ as recipe steps are completed)

... Stage 1 in bucket — finishes ... (date) (List anything special to remember, e.g. remove mould after X days.)

... Stage 2 in fermentation demi-john — finishes ... (date) (Note down dates and amounts of any extra feeding required.)

... Stage 3 racking and clearing 1st rack ... (date): 2nd ... (date) etc. (Note date each time you rack, whether still cloudy, etc.)

... Stage 4 bottling

Remarks

(Space for anything you notice which may be helpful another time you make the wine. E.g.: very lively — next time leave more room in demi-john until fermentation has died down a little.)

Assessment after drinking

	Comments
1st bottle drunk (date): ...	Just drinkable
2nd ...	Still a little sweet
3rd ...	Very good
4th ...	Ditto
etc.	

Some people judge their wines on colour, bouquet, taste and strength and give them a comparative score out of ten. I personally find that it is adequate simply to mark down horrible!/just drinkable/very good/excellent, etc. Commenting on each bottle is invaluable research for future makings so that you will know just how long it is best kept before drinking.

PART II
WINES

WINES AS REMEDIES

Years ago, many people depended almost entirely on home-made remedies for their ailments. Quite a number of country people today still believe in them implicitly. Wines are quite important in this role and are a very pleasant way of taking medicine. I am sure if doctors' medicines were so delicious, the Health Service would collapse entirely!

Here are some wines which are, so I am told, safe and certain cures. Anyway a glass of wine at any time can be a great morale lifter and may help one to forget one's aches and pains. I must, however, warn those who suffer from rheumatism, that they should never touch rhubarb wine.

Cowslip wine will cure jaundice.
Dandelion is good for indigestion and kidney trouble.
Sloe wine may be effective for diarrhoea.
Elderberry wine taken hot on a cold morning will ward off colds.
Raspberry wine is invaluable for sore throats.
Blackcurrant wine when mulled is excellent for colds and bronchitis.
Barley wine is good for kidney trouble.
And Rhubarb wine is bad for rheumatism.

A CALENDAR FOR WINEMAKING

It is often hard, especially if one happens to live in a town, to remember when the time is for making various wines. People who live in the country are more fortunate as they can see when the different flowers and fruits are ready.

This calendar will act as a reminder. Town folk on a fine

25

day can pack their lunch and sally forth to the country in search of the fruits and flowers of the fields and hedgerows. The country folk can just step outside their doors any day and help themselves, to the wild flowers and fruits at least: not, I hope, to the farmer's wheat or sugar beet!

There are wines to make in every month, plenty to keep the most industrious person busy, but I don't think many people could find the storage space for so many different varieties. However, if you can only try a few, there should be enough to ensure a Merry Christmas.

The dried fruit wines can, of course, be made all the year round. I have only included them in the winter months when there are not so many varieties of fruit and vegetables to be found.

The weather influences the season of the flowers and fruits. In a cold year they may be late, and in a warm year a bit earlier, but it doesn't vary more than a week or so. Some things such as grapes and pears can be bought at any time in the shops, but the out-of-season varieties are too expensive for wine.

In general pick flowers in full bloom, fruits ripe, and vegetables ready to eat.

WINE CALENDAR

January

Potato, Wheat, Barley, Raisin, Ginger, Fig, Dried Apricot, Dried Peach, Orange.

February

Potato, Wheat, Barley, Raisin, Lemon, Fig, Parsnip, Dried Apricot, Dried Peach, Ginger.

March

Coltsfoot, Lemon, Tea, Parsnip, Turnip, Potato, Carrot, Barley, Dried Fruits.

April
Dandelion, Parsnip, Turnip, Carrot, Tea, Ginger, Dried Fruits.

May
Dandelion, Rhubarb, Marigold, Cowslip, Elderflower, Gooseberry.

June
Strawberry, Marigold, Dandelion, Elderflower, Rhubarb, Gooseberry, Plum.

July
Blackcurrant, Redcurrant, Raspberry, Cherry, Clove Carnation, Plum, Bullace.

August
Peach, Apricot, Loganberry, Pear, Plum, Grape, Bullace, Clove Carnation, Marigold, Mulberry, Damson.

September
Grape, Pear, Plum, Damson, Blackberry, Carrot, Beetroot, Marrow, Quince, Mulberry, Elderberry.

October
Apple, Blackberry, Hip, Haw, Grape, Sloe, Sugar Beet, Marrow, Carrot, Elderberry, Turnip, Quince, Beetroot.

November
Apple, Sugar Beet, Marrow, Mangel, Potato, Orange, Wheat, Barley, Carrot, Lemon, Tea.

December
Orange, Lemon, Rice, Apple, Tea, Wheat, Barley, Raisin, Dried Apricot, Dried Peach, Fig, Ginger.

PART III
WINE RECIPES

APPLE WINE

> 3½ lb. cooking apples.
> 2½ lb. granulated sugar.
> 6 pts cold water.
> 2 lemons.
> 1 orange.
> Campden tablets.
> G.P. wine yeast.
> Yeast nutrient.
> Pectic enzyme.

WASH the apples and cut out any bad places. Do not peel or core but cut the apples into pieces and put them through the mincer. Now put the minced apples in a sterile plastic bucket and pour 6 pts. of cold water over them.

Add the 2½ lb. of granulated sugar and the juice and grated rind (remove pith) of the two lemons and one orange. Stir well until the sugar has dissolved. Put in the pectic enzyme and one crushed campden tablet, cover and leave for 24 hours in a warm place, then add yeast, yeast nutrient, stir, re-cover and leave for one week but remember to stir well each day.

It will then be ready to strain and put into a fermentation demi-john. Fit an airlock and leave to ferment out. Rack, allow to clear and bottle.

If you can leave it for four months you will find it has turned into a very, pleasant tasting wine.

FRESH APRICOT WINE

> 4 lb. fresh apricots
> (weigh after stoning).
> 3 lb. granulated sugar.
> 6 pts. boiling water.
> Campden tablets.
> G.P. wine yeast.
> Yeast nutrient.
> Pectic enzyme.

Stone the apricots, cut them into small pieces, and place these in a plastic bucket. Add sugar.

Pour the boiling water over and stir well. Cover. When sufficiently cool add pectic enzyme and a crushed campden tablet to the must. Leave covered in a warm place for 24 hours before adding yeast and yeast nutrient. Allow to ferment in the covered bucket for five days, stirring well each day. Strain through muslin into another plastic bucket, cover and leave for three to four more days in the warm.

The wine is now ready to go into a fermentation demi-john. Fit an airlock and re-place in the warm until fermentation is finished. Rack into another demi-john, into which a campden tablet has been crushed, to clear before bottling.

Taste the wine now and again, and if you think it needs some more sugar it won't hurt to add a little.

Store in a cool, dark place and leave for at least six months before drinking.

DRIED APRICOT WINE

> 2 lb. dried apricots.
> 3 lb. granulated sugar.
> 1 gallon water.
> Pectic enzyme.
> Campden tablets.
> G.P. wine yeast.
> Yeast nutrient.

Wash the 2 lbs. of dried apricots, place in a large bowl with the water, cover and leave to soak for 24 hours.

Put the apricots and water into a large preserving pan or saucepan and bring to the boil. Simmer till tender.

Return the mixture to your large bowl or plastic bucket and add the sugar, stirring well to make sure it dissolves. Allow to cool sufficiently, add a crushed campden tablet and the pectic enzyme. Leave for 24 hours in a warm place, properly covered, then add the yeast and yeast nutrient.

Re-cover and keep in a warm place for five days not forgetting to stir daily. This allows the wine to ferment on the fruit and afterwards the wine is ready to strain into a demi-john. Fit with an airlock and leave to ferment.

Each week add a tablespoonful of sugar to the demi-john until the wine has fermented out. This process is known as feeding the wine (see page 14/15).

After fermentation has ceased the wine is ready to rack, clear, and bottle as usual. Ready to drink in nine months.

The apricots left after straining off the liquid will make jam* if about 4 or 5 lb of sugar is added. Make as usual for dried apricot jam, adding more water, of course.

* *Publishers' note:* Readers may like to refer to 'The Right Way to Make Jams' by Cyril Grange, in the *Right Way* series published by Elliot Right Way Books.

BARLEY WINE

1½ lb. barley.
3 lb. granulated sugar.
1½ gallons cold water.
½ teaspoon ground ginger.
1 lemon.
1 orange.
Prepared juice of ½ lb. raisins.
½ cup cold strong tea.
Campden tablets.
G.P. wine yeast.
Yeast nutrient.

Prepare the raisin juice as explained under 'preparation' page 18. Put the barley into a large saucepan or preserving pan, and pour on 1½ gallons of cold water. Place over heat and bring to the boil. Simmer for about half an hour, then strain through muslin into a plastic bucket.

Remove the pith and add the lemon and orange juices and skins, the 3 lb. granulated sugar and ½ teaspoon ground ginger. Pour in the raisin juice and cold tea. Stir well until the sugar has dissolved. Add a crushed campden tablet and leave for 24 hours, then stir in yeast and yeast nutrient.

Cover the bucket and leave in a ROOM temperature of around 70°F (20°C) for ten to fourteen days, then strain into a fermentation demi-john and fit an airlock. This wine will need feeding occasionally with sugar; put a tablespoonful in every week or so. Continue to keep it in the warm place.

When the fermentation has ceased, rack into another jar and allow to clear before bottling. You can drink the wine after six months, but it improves with age. Keep it a year or so and it will be a wine really worth drinking.

BEETROOT WINE

> 3 lb. beetroot.
> 3lb. granulated sugar.
> 1 gallon cold water.
> Prepared juice of ½ lb raisins
> 1 lemon.
> 1 orange.
> 6 cloves.
> Pectic enzyme.
> Campden tablets.
> G.P. wine yeast.
> Yeast nutrient.

Prepare your raisin juice in advance as explained in part I, 'preparation'.

Wash the beetroot well, but do not peel. Cut it into thin slices and put into a saucepan or preserving pan with the 1 gallon of water. Bring it to the boil and simmer until the beetroot is tender but not mashy.

Strain off the liquid, and throw away the beetroot, or remove the skin and cover with pepper, salt and vinegar and eat it. Put the liquid back into the saucepan, add the prepared raisin juice plus juice and skins (not the pith) of the fruit, the 3 lb. sugar and six cloves and heat just enough to melt the sugar: stir well all the time.

Let the liquid cool right down, then pour it into a sterile plastic bucket. Add a crushed campden tablet and pectic enzyme and leave covered in a warm surrounding for 24 hours. Then add the yeast and yeast nutrient. Cover the bucket carefully and leave for three days, stirring daily. Strain the wine into a fermentation demi-john and ferment through an airlock until dry. When fermentation has finished, rack into another demi-john to clear before bottling.

It should be ready to drink in six months, but the longer you keep it the better it will be.

BLACKBERRY WINE (BRAMBLE)

3 lb. blackberries.
3 lb. granulated sugar.
6 pts. boiling water.
Campden tablets.
G.P. wine yeast.
Yeast nutrient.
Pectic enzyme.

Gather the fruit when ripe on a dry sunny day. Wash the berries to remove any maggots which so often get into the blackberries.

Place the blackberries in a large plastic bucket and pour over the six pints of boiling water. Add the sugar and stir well; cover and leave to cool right down. Add the pectic enzyme and a crushed campden tablet and leave for 24 hours, once again covered over in a warm place. Then add the yeast and the yeast nutrient and leave for seven days. Remember to stir each day and to keep the bucket in a warm place.

Strain the liquid off carefully through muslin or using a straining bag making sure that no pips or pulp get through to the demi-john. Fit an airlock and allow fermentation to continue until dryness. The wine is now ready to rack, clear and bottle in the usual way. It should be ready to drink in six months and it is a lovely dark red wine which is rather sweet. If you can add a glass of port or ruby wine to the bottle just before drinking, the flavour is greatly enhanced.

BLACKCURRANT WINE

> 4 lb. blackcurrants.
> 3 lb. granulated sugar.
> 6 pts. cold water.
> Campden tablets.
> G.P. wine yeast.
> Yeast nutrient.
> Pectic enzyme.

Strip the blackcurrants from the stalks and wash them carefully so as not to lose too much of the juice.

Put them in a plastic bucket and crush them well using a plastic spoon. Pour on the six pints of cold water, add the sugar, the pectic enzyme and a crushed campden tablet and stir thoroughly. Leave covered in a warm place for 24 hours; then add yeast and yeast nutrient.

Re-cover the bucket and leave for ten days, but no longer. Stir daily and make sure the room remains warm. Then strain into a fermentation demi-john, fit an airlock, allow to ferment out and rack, clear and bottle as usual.

Ready in six months.

ANOTHER METHOD

Some people prefer to make this wine with boiling water. Use the same ingredients and quantities.

Wash the fruit and put it into a plastic bucket but do not crush it. Pour on six pints of boiling water and allow to cool to 70°F (20°C) before continuing with the recipe exactly as in the cold water recipe above.

BULLACE PLUM WINE

4 lb. bullaces.
3 lb. granulated sugar.
6 pts. cold water.
Campden tablets.
G.P. wine yeast.
Yeast nutrient.
Pectic enzyme.

Bullaces are best when picked after a frost. Wash the fruit remove the stones and place it in a plastic bucket.

Pour the cold water over the fruit and stir well with a plastic spoon.

Cover the bucket and leave for about three weeks *without further stirring* so that the thick mould which forms is not disturbed. A warm room will be the best place while the mould forms.

Remove the mould carefully, in one piece if possible. Try to avoid little pieces breaking off into the wine. Then strain the liquid off into another plastic bucket. Now the pectic enzyme, crushed campden tablet and sugar go in and you leave the mixture covered for 24 hours before adding the yeast and the yeast nutrient. Cover the bucket again and leave for three days in a warm atmosphere, stirring daily.

The wine is now ready to strain into the fermentation demi-john and to ferment to dryness. After that it can be racked and cleared and then bottled in the usual manner. Store in a cool dark place and try to leave this wine at least a year before drinking, as it needs longer to mature than some wines.

Forming a mould in the process of wine making was an important part of the process in bygone days. This method combines the old-fashioned and tested procedure with more modern methods, equipment and scientific additives. It is included not only for the fine taste of the wine but for the fun of seeing how wine used to be made.

Although looking at the mould may be a very unpleasant experience and it does not seem possible that this horrible concoction can turn into a clear refreshing wine, I can assure you it can, so do not be discouraged!

CARROT WINE

4 lb. carrots.
3 lb. granulated sugar.
1 gallon cold water.
½ oz. hops.
Prepared juice of ½ lb.
raisins.
1 orange.
1 lemon.
Pectic enzyme.
Campden tablets.
G.P. wine yeast.
Yeast nutrient.

Scrub the carrots well and cut them into pieces. Put them in a large preserving pan or saucepan with a gallon of cold water. Boil until the carrots are tender, then strain off the liquid into a plastic bucket. Remove the carrots, then pour the liquid back into the pan and add 3 lb. of granulated sugar and ½ oz. hops. Stir well and just bring to the boil.

Strain into a bucket through muslin to remove the hops, and leave until sufficiently cool for the pectic enzyme and crushed campden tablet to be added. Leave covered in a warm place for 24 hours, before adding juice and rind (no pith) of lemon and orange, prepared raisin juice (see part 1 "preparation"), followed by yeast and yeast nutrient. Recover and allow to ferment for a week, stirring twice daily. Keep the bucket covered.

Strain into a fermentation demi-john, fit airlock, keep in the warm and ferment until dry. This may need feeding with a tablespoon of sugar at intervals during the fermentation. When fermentation has finished, rack into another demi-john and allow to clear before bottling.

It will be drinkable in six months, but keep it longer if you can.

CHERRY WINE

5 lb. ripe black cherries.
3 lb. granulated sugar.
1 gallon cold water.
Pectic enzyme.
Campden tablets.
G.P. wine yeast.
Yeast nutrient.

Remove the stalks and stones from the cherries and wash the fruit. Place the cherries in a large saucepan or preserving pan and crush them with a plastic spoon.

Pour on a gallon of cold water and bring them to the boil. Simmer gently until the cherries are tender, then remove from the heat and strain the liquid off through muslin into a plastic bucket. When you have strained off all the liquid, tip the cherries themselves into the muslin, and squeeze gently to extract any remaining juice, taking care not to scald yourself.

Add the 3 lb. of granulated sugar and stir well so that the sugar dissolves. Allow to cool right down and add pectic enzyme and a crushed campden tablet, then cover and leave for 24 hours before putting in yeast and yeast nutrient. Then cover the bucket and leave for three days in a warm room stirring daily.

Transfer now into a fermentation demi-john, fit an airlock, keeping in the warm and ferment until dry. When fermentation has finished, rack into another demi-john into which a crushed campden tablet has been put and allow to clear before bottling.

You can drink it in six months' time, but keep it longer if you can.

CLOVE CARNATION WINE

2 quarts clove carnations.
3 lb. granulated sugar.
6 pts. boiling water.
½ cup of cold strong tea.
1 lemon
1 orange.
Campden tablets.
G.P. wine yeast.
Yeast nutrient.

Pick the carnations, the clove scented kind, on a sunny day. Use only the heads of the flowers, and wash them well to remove any insects. Measure them in a quart jug. You need two jugs full.

Put the carnation heads into a plastic bucket and pour over the boiling water. Add sugar, stir well, and allow to cool right off. Take the juice and rinds but not the pith of the fruit and add in to the mixture together with a crushed campden tablet and pour in the cold tea. Cover and put in a warm atmosphere for 24 hours, then add the yeast and yeast nutrient. Re-cover and keep in the warm atmosphere for ten days, stirring well daily. When stirring it is important to macerate the flower heads as explained under preparation, page 18.

Strain into a fermentation demi-john, fit airlock, place in the warm and ferment until dry. When fermentation has finished, rack and clear before bottling.

If the wine turns out too dry sweeten with non-fermenting sugar.

Keep this wine at least nine months before drinking.

COLTSFOOT WINE

2 quarts of coltsfoot flowers.
3 lb. granulated sugar.
6pts. boiling water.
Prepared juice of ½ lb. raisins.
1 lemon.
½ cup cold strong tea.
Campden tablets
G.P. wine yeast.
Yeast nutrient.

Prepare your raisin juice in advance as described in part 1, 'preparation'.

Pick the flowers on a sunny day and measure the coltsfoot while fresh. Shake them well and wash to remove any insects. Put them in a plastic bucket and pour on the six pints boiling water. Stir well and macerate the flowers, then cover the bucket and leave for four days.

Now strain the liquid off into a large saucepan or preserving pan. Add the lemon juice and skin having removed the pith. Bring it just to the boil, remove from the heat and add the sugar, stirring till dissolved.

Pour it all into a plastic bucket along with the prepared raisin juice and the cold tea and leave until the temperature has dropped to around 70°F (20°C); then add a crushed campden tablet, cover and leave for 24 hours in a warm room. Then stir in the yeast and yeast nutrient.

Cover the bucket but stir daily for three more days. Then strain into a fermentation demi-john, fit airlock, place in the warm and ferment until dry. When fermentation has finished, rack into another demi-john to clear before bottling. Sweeten if necessary before drinking. Use a non-fermenting sweetener.

Ready to drink in six months, but it will improve if you can keep it longer.

COWSLIP WINE

> 2 quarts cowslip flowers.
> 3 lb. granulated sugar.
> 6 pts. boiling water.
> 1 lemon.
> ½ cup cold strong tea.
> Campden tablets.
> G.P. wine yeast.
> Yeast nutrient.

Pick the flowers on a dry day; only the heads are used. Measure them into a quart jug, but don't press them down.

When you have measured two jugs full, wash the flowers well and place in a plastic bucket.

Pour the boiling water on them, add the sugar, stir well remembering to macerate the flowers, then add the lemon juice and rind (having removed pith) plus the cold tea; cover the bucket and leave to get cold. Then add campden tablet (crushed) and keep in a warm room for 24 hours. Now the yeast and yeast nutrient go in and you cover and keep in the warm for seven days, stirring daily.

Strain into a fermentation demi-john fitted with an airlock and ferment until dry. You may find that it needs a little feeding during fermentation as explained under 'using the fermentation demi-john' — a tablespoonful or two each week should be enough.

This can be drunk at once, but will improve with keeping.

Nature conservationists will want to go easy on quantities of Cowslip wine as the pretty yellow flowers have been decreasing rapidly in recent years and their reproduction depends on the seeds which you are destroying. Therefore, be quite sure that authority has been given for you to pick them.

DAMSON WINE. FIRST METHOD

3 lb. ripe damsons.
3 lb. granulated sugar.
6 pts. cold water.
Pectic enzyme.
Campden tablets.
G.P. wine yeast.
Yeast nutrient.

Choose ripe damsons, wash them, remove the stones and

place in a plastic bucket. Pour over cold water and stir with a plastic spoon. Now cover the bucket and leave until a thick mould has formed on top. This may take weeks, but it doesn't matter as long as you keep the bucket covered. The flavour of the wine will be better if there is a good thick mould. See Bullace Plum Wine for notes on mould.

When you are satisfied that the mould is thick enough, remove it carefully, in one piece if possible. Strain the liquid off into another bucket and add 3 lb. of granulated sugar, a crushed campden tablet and the pectic enzyme, stir well with a plastic spoon until the sugar has dissolved.

Cover the bucket and leave for 24 hours; then put in yeast and yeast nutrient, re-cover and leave in the warm for three more days, stirring each day. Strain into a fermentation demi-john, keep in the warm and ferment until dry. Rack into another demi-john to clear before bottling.

You can drink it in six months, but it will improve in flavour if you can keep it longer.

DAMSON WINE. SECOND METHOD

3 lb. ripe damsons.
3 lb. granulated sugar.
1 gallon cold water.
Pectic enzyme.
Campden tablets.
G.P. wine yeast.
Yeast nutrient.

Pick or buy the damsons as ripe as possible, remove stones and wash them well. Put the 3 lb. damsons in a large saucepan or preserving pan, and pour on a gallon of cold water.

43

Bring to the boil and simmer until the damsons are tender but not mashy. Strain off the liquid through muslin into a plastic bucket. The damsons can now be used as stewed fruit or for making jam.

Add 3 lb. of granulated sugar to the liquid in the bucket and stir well with a plastic spoon until the sugar has dissolved. Leave to cool right down, then add pectic enzyme and a crushed campden tablet. Allow 24 hours covered in a warm atmosphere before stirring in the yeast and yeast nutrient. Then leave in the warm for three days before you transfer into a fermentation demi-john, fit an airlock and ferment until dry. When the fermentation has stopped, rack and clear before bottling. Some feeding may be required during fermentation and a tablespoonful of sugar added once or twice should do no harm.

You will be able to drink it in six months or perhaps before that. But, the longer you keep it the better it will be.

DANDELION WINE

2 quarts dandelion flowers.
3 lb. granulated sugar.
1 lemon.
1 orange.
½ cup strong cold tea.
6 pts. boiling water.
Campden tablets.
G.P. wine yeast.
Yeast nutrient.

Pick the dandelions on a fine day when the flowers are open. Pick the heads off and measure two quart jugs full.

To remove any insects wash the flowers and then put them

44

in a plastic bucket. Take the juice and rinds of the fruit (no pith) and add to the flowerheads along with the cold tea.

Pour over the six pints of boiling water, stir well and macerate. Once cool add a crushed campden tablet. Cover the bucket and leave in a warm surrounding for ten days, but no longer.

Now strain the liquid off into another bucket and stir in 3 lb. of granulated sugar and the yeast and yeast nutrient. Cover the bucket and leave for another three days in the warm.

Strain into a fermentation demi-john fit an airlock and ferment until dry. You can add a little sugar after a week or two if fermentation seems slow. Rack and clear in the normal way before bottling.

This wine is very nice when new, but it will improve with age.

ELDERBERRY WINE. FIRST METHOD

> 5 lb. elderberries.
> 3 lb. granulated sugar.
> 1 gallon cold water.
> 6 cloves.
> Pectic enzyme.
> Campden tablets.
> ½ teaspoon of ground ginger.
> G.P. wine yeast.
> Yeast nutrient.

Gather 5lb. of elderberries: there are always plenty in the hedgerows. Strip the berries from the stalks; this is easiest to do with a fork; slide it down the stems and push the berries off.

Wash the fruit well, and put it in a preserving pan with a gallon of cold water. Boil until the fruit is tender, then strain off the liquid into a plastic bucket.

Add 3 lb. granulated sugar, six cloves, the ground ginger, and stir well to dissolve the sugar and ginger. When the liquid is sufficiently cool add a crushed campden tablet and pectic enzyme, cover and leave for 24 hours in a warm room. Then add yeast and yeast nutrient.

Cover the bucket and leave in the warm for ten days stirring daily, then strain into a demi-john; fit an airlock and keep in the warm while the mixture ferments to dryness. The wine can then be racked and bottled in the usual way.

This wine is very good for colds, especially when taken hot.

It is ready in six months, but better if left longer.

ELDERBERRY WINE. SECOND METHOD

4 lb. elderberries.
3 lb. granulated sugar.
6 pts. boiling water.
3 cloves.
Prepared juice of ½ lb. raisins.
A pinch of ground ginger.
Pectic enzyme.
Campden tablets.
G.P. wine yeast.
Yeast nutrient.

Prepare your raisin juice in advance (see part 1, 'preparation').

Pick and wash 4lb. of elderberries. Strip them from the stalks and place in a plastic bucket. Add the raisin juice and pour over a gallon of boiling water, and stir well. Cover the bucket and leave for two weeks. Stir daily.

Now strain off the liquid into a saucepan and add three cloves and the pinch of ground ginger. Just bring it to the boil, and then pour it over the 3 lb. of granulated sugar in a bucket. Stir well to dissolve the sugar and ginger. Allow to cool right down and add a crushed campden tablet and the pectic enzyme. Leave covered in warm surroundings for 24 hours before putting yeast and yeast nutrient in. Cover and keep in the warm for three more days, stirring daily.

The wine is then ready to strain and ferment out in the demi-john with an airlock fitted. When fermentation has finished, rack into another demi-john and allow to clear before bottling.

Ready to drink in six months, but it is much better if kept over a year.

ELDERFLOWER WINE

1 pint elderflowers.
3 lb. granulated sugar.
6 pts. boiling water.
1 lemon.
1 orange.
½ cup cold strong tea.
Campden tablets.
G.P. wine yeast.
Yeast nutrient.

After you have cut off the stalks, measure a pint of elderflowers. Wash the flowers to remove insects, then put them in a plastic bucket with the juice and grated rind of the lemon and orange, (no pith) and the cold tea.

Now pour over the boiling water and stir well with a plastic spoon. Cover the bucket and leave it in a warm place for four days. Then strain the liquid off into a saucepan and just bring it to the boil. Put 3 lb. of granulated sugar in a bucket and pour the boiling liquid over; stir well until the sugar has dissolved. When the liquid is sufficiently cool add a crushed campden tablet; wait 24 hours and add the yeast and yeast nutrient.

Cover the bucket well, and leave for another six days, stirring daily. After this time, transfer to an airlocked demi-john and ferment until dry. When fermentation has finished, rack into another demi-john and allow to clear before bottling. Feed in a tablespoon or two of sugar during fermentation but take care not to add sugar once the yeast is used up and no further reaction can be seen.

Ready to drink in six months.

FIG WINE

2 lb. dried figs.
2½ lb. brown sugar.
6 pts. boiling water.
Prepared juice of ½ lb.
large raisins.
1 lemon.
1 orange.
A pinch of ground ginger.
Campden tablets.
Pectic enzyme.
G.P. wine yeast.
Yeast nutrient.

Cut the figs into small pieces and place in a plastic bucket, with the $2\frac{1}{2}$ lb. brown sugar. Add the raisin juice (see part 1, 'preparation') to the figs. Add the pinch of ground ginger, the grated rinds of the lemon and orange and the juice, but no pith or pips. Then pour on six pints of boiling water and stir well with a plastic spoon.

When the mixture is lukewarm put in the pectic enzyme and a crushed campden tablet and leave covered where the ROOM temperature is around 70°F (20°C) for 24 hours, then stir in the yeast and yeast nutrient. Cover the bucket and leave for twelve days, but stir daily.

After twelve days it is ready to strain into a demi-john. Keep in the warm with an airlock fitted until fermentation has finished, rack and clear before bottling.

It is ready to drink in six months, but will improve with age. If the wine is too dry, sweeten to taste.

GINGER WINE

2½ oz. root ginger.
3 lb. granulated sugar.
10 pts. of water.
2 tablespoons of honey.
Juice of three lemons.
Campden tablets.
G.P. wine yeast.
Yeast nutrient.

Bruise the root ginger well (you may find this easier once it has softened — so read on!) and put it in a saucepan with three pints of the water. Bring to the boil and simmer for half an hour. Into a large plastic bucket put 3 lb. of granulated sugar, the juice of three lemons, and two tablespoons of honey. Pour the ginger and water on to this and stir well. Boil the remainder of the water and add to the other ingredients, stir it all well, then pop in a crushed campden tablet and cover and leave for 24 hours. Stir in yeast and yeast nutrient and leave in a warm place for a further 24 hours.

It is ready to strain into a fermentation demi-john without further ado, fit an airlock and allow to ferment to dryness. When fermentation has finished, rack and clear before bottling. You can drink it at once.

I don't waste the root ginger; I put it back into the saucepan with ½ lb. of sugar and a pint of water and boil until the liquid is reduced to syrup. This is useful either to add to hot drinks, or to use as flavouring in puddings or cakes.

GOOSEBERRY WINE. FIRST METHOD

3 lb. ripe gooseberries.
3 lb. granulated sugar.
6 pts. boiling water.
2 heads of elderflowers.
Pectic enzyme.
Campden tablets.
G.P. wine yeast.
Yeast nutrient.

Wash the gooseberries and put them in a plastic bucket. Mash them with a plastic spoon, add the elderflower heads and the sugar, then pour on the boiling water. Stir well, then re-cover the bucket and allow to cool right off. Now add the campden tablet (crushed) and the pectic enzyme and leave in a warm place covered over for 24 hours. Then put in the yeast and the yeast nutrient, re-cover and leave in the warm surroundings for ten days, stirring well each day.

It is then ready to strain into a fermentation demi-john, fit an airlock and ferment to dryness. Rack into another demi-john and allow to clear before bottling. Note that with this wine especially, it is a mistake to allow the wine to sit on any sediment during the clearing process for more than four weeks. Always re-rack if necessary.

Keep in a dark cool place for at least six months before drinking and longer if you can.

In this recipe the two heads of elderflower are added in order to produce a fine bouquet as described on page 19.

GOOSEBERRY WINE. SECOND METHOD

6 lb. ripe gooseberries.
3 lb. granulated sugar.
6 pts. boiling water.
Prepared juice of ½ lb. raisins.
Pectic enzyme.
Campden tablets.
G.P. wine yeast.
Yeast nutrient.

Prepare your raisin juice in advance as explained in part 1, 'preparation'.

Wash the gooseberries and mash or cut them up into a plastic bucket. Add the raisin juice to the gooseberries. Add the 3 lb. of granulated sugar and pour over the boiling water, and stir well.

When the mixture is lukewarm add a crushed campden tablet and the pectic enzyme and leave covered in the warm for 24 hours; then stir in the yeast and yeast nutrient. Leave for ten days, stirring every day, always replacing the cover with great care and making sure the room stays warm.

After ten days strain off the liquid into a fermentation demi-john with airlock and keep in the warm until fermentation has finished. Rack and allow to clear before bottling.

The wine should be ready to drink in six months, but keep it longer if possible! Sweeten to taste if necessary.

GRAPE WINE

3½ lb. green grapes.
1 lb. black grapes.
3 lb. granulated sugar.
6 pts. boiling water.
Campden tablets.
Pectic enzyme.
G.P. wine yeast.
Yeast nutrient.

Wash the grapes well and put them into a plastic bucket. Crush the grapes with your hands or a plastic spoon so as not to break the pips. Pour over the six pints of boiling water, add the sugar and stir well. As soon as the must has cooled right down add a crushed campden tablet and your pectic enzyme. Cover and place the bucket in a warm position for 24 hours, then stir in the yeast and yeast nutrient. Cover the bucket and leave it for ten days, stirring daily.

After ten days it is then ready to strain into a fermentation demi-john. Fit an airlock and keep in the warm until fermentation has finished. Do not leave the wine on the sediment for more than four weeks. Rack into another demi-john, keep in a cool place for the wine to clear before bottling. Leave it for at least six months and much longer if you can, as grape wine improves with age.

UNRIPE GRAPE WINE

3 lb. unripe grapes.
Prepared juice of 1 lb. raisins.
2 lb. granulated sugar.
1 lb. demerara sugar.
6 pts. boiling water.
Campden tablets.
Pectic enzyme.
G.P. wine yeast.
Yeast nutrient.

I expect many of you who have grape vines find that in bad summers the grapes will not ripen. There is no need to waste them, as they make a really nice wine. I always use mine this way. Prepare your raisin juice ahead, see part 1, 'preparation'.

Crush the grapes with the hands, or very carefully with a plastic spoon so as not to break the pips. Put them into a plastic bucket, add the raisin juice. Pour on the six pints of boiling water and add all the sugar; stir well to dissolve. Allow to cool sufficiently and pop in a crushed campden tablet and the pectic enzyme. After 24 hours in the warm you can add yeast and yeast nutrient. Cover the bucket and leave it in the warm for ten days, stirring every day.

It is now ready to strain into a fermentation demi-john

and fit an airlock so that it can continue to ferment out to dryness in the usual way. Taste it after fermentation has stopped and if it seems a little sour, add some non-fermenting sweetener. Then rack, allow to clear and bottle.

This wine will take nine months at least to mature, but try to leave it longer.

GREENGAGE WINE

3½ lb. over-ripe greengages.
3 lb. granulated sugar.
6 pts. of boiling water.
Pectic enzyme.
Campden tablets.
G.P. wine yeast.
Yeast nutrient.

Wash the greengages, remove the stones and put them in a plastic bucket. It does not matter if some of them are a bit squashy; they need to be over-ripe to make good wine.

Pour the six pints of boiling water over the greengages, add the sugar and stir the whole mixture well. Then cover the bucket and allow it to cool before putting in a crushed campden tablet and the pectic enzyme. Leave in a warm place for 24 hours; then put in the yeast and the yeast nutrient. Cover again and keep in the warm place for ten days, stirring each day.

After this time the mixture is ready to strain into a demi-john, fit an airlock and allow to ferment out. Rack, allow to clear and bottle in the usual way.

The wine is ready to drink in six months but, like most wines, it improves with longer keeping. If it is too dry you can always sweeten a little with sugar before drinking.

HAW WINE

6 lb. haws.
3 lb. granulated sugar.
6 pts boiling water.
Pectic enzyme.
Campden tablets.
G.P. wine yeast.
Yeast nutrient.

Pick six pounds of haws; this will not be difficult as there are plenty about in the Autumn. Choose ripe ones.

Wash the haws well and cut off the stalks. Put them in a plastic bucket and pour the boiling water over them, add the sugar, stir well, and try to mash them a little with a plastic spoon. As soon as the must has cooled off a crushed campden tablet and the pectic enzyme must go in. Then wait 24 hours, leaving the bucket covered and in a warm room, before adding yeast and yeast nutrient. Then cover the bucket and leave for ten days, stirring daily.

The wine is then ready to strain into a fermentation demi-john, fit an airlock, and place it in the warm to ferment until dry. Rack into another demi-john to clear before bottling.

You can drink it after six months, but keep it longer if possible. Sweeten to taste if necessary.

HIP WINE

> 3½ lb. rose hips.
> 3 lb. granulated sugar.
> 6 pts. cold water.

This is a really economical wine as the only major ingredient to be bought is the sugar. There are always plenty of hips in the hedgerows; they also contain a large amount of Vitamin C, which I should think would be retained in the wine.

Wash the rose hips and cut them in half; put them in a plastic bucket and pour on the six pints of cold water. Stir them well with a plastic spoon, then cover the bucket and leave them for two weeks.

After two weeks, strain off the liquid into another bucket and add the 3 lb. of granulated sugar. Stir until it has dissolved. Cover the bucket and leave for five days, stirring daily. Because the recipe depends on the natural yeast available from the rose hips it is even more essential than usual to keep the bucket in a room with a steady warm temperature around 70°F (20°C). Without warmth the yeast will not do its work efficiently.

The wine is then ready to be strained into a fermentation demi-john, fitted with an airlock, and put in a warm place to complete fermentation to dryness.

Rack and clear before bottling.

The wine should be ready to drink in six months, but keep it longer if you can.

As explained in the preface this recipe follows Mrs. Gennery-Taylor's original method faithfully (except that in those days fermenting was allowed to continue in the bottles — loosely corked till it had ceased!).

Should you have any worries over the wine clearing itself, or becoming infected, you can 'cheat' a little by adding a crushed campden tablet and pectic enzyme when you first rack it.

LEMON WINE

6 lemons.
3 lb. granulated sugar.
1 gallon cold water.
Prepared juice of ½ lb. raisins.
Pectic enzyme.
Campden tablets.
G.P. wine yeast.
Yeast nutrient.

Prepare your raisin juice (see part 1, 'preparation').

Wash the lemons, and peel off the yellow rind very thinly so as not to get any pith left on it. Put the rind into a large saucepan or preserving pan with a gallon of cold water, bring it to the boil and simmer for twenty minutes.

Squeeze the juice from the lemons into a plastic bucket containing the 3 lb. of sugar and the prepared raisin juice. Strain the water off the lemon peel on to the sugar and raisins. Stir well with a plastic spoon until the sugar has dissolved.

When cool, stir in the pectic enzyme and a crushed campden tablet. Cover and leave for 24 hours in warm surroundings; then add yeast and yeast nutrient.

Cover the bucket and leave it to stand for seven days in a warm place, but stir daily. Then strain it through a piece of muslin into a fermentation demi-john to ferment through the airlock. To aid the fermentation process you may need to add one or two tablespoonfuls of sugar once or twice. When the fermentation has finished, rack and clear before bottling.

It will be ready to drink in about six months, but try and keep it longer.

LOGANBERRY WINE

$3\frac{1}{2}$ lb. loganberries.
3 lb. granulated sugar.
6 pts. boiling water.
Pectic enzyme.
Campden tablets.
G.P. wine yeast.
Yeast nutrient.

Pick the loganberries and wash them well, but do it carefully so as not to lose too much of the juice. Put them in a plastic bucket and pour on the six pints of boiling water, add the sugar and stir well mashing the berries with a plastic spoon. Cover the bucket and leave it to cool right down. Pop in a crushed campden tablet and the pectic enzyme then leave in a warm atmosphere for 24 hours. Add the yeast and yeast nutrient and leave it for ten days but stir at least once per day.

After ten days it can be strained into a fermentation demijohn. Fit an airlock and keep in the warm to ferment until dry. Rack and clear before bottling.

It should be ready to drink in about six months, but if you want a really good wine leave it at least a year. You can, if you wish, add a little non-fermenting sweetener to taste.

MANGEL OR MANGOLD WINE

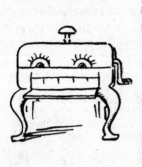

> 4 lb. mangels.
> 3 lb. demerara sugar.
> 1 gallon cold water.
> Prepared juice of ½ lb. raisins.
> 1 orange.
> Pectic enzyme.
> Campden tablets.
> G.P. wine yeast.
> Yeast nutrient.

You need the humble mangel wurzel or mangold which anyone living in the country should be able to obtain easily enough. Wait until the mangels have had a frost on them as they will make a better wine. Prepare your raisin juice ahead as explained in part 1, 'preparation'.

Wash the mangels well, but do not peel them. Slice them thinly into a large saucepan or preserving pan, with 1 gallon of cold water, or as much water as you can get in. If the pan is not big enough to hold 1 gallon, add some later as the water evaporates.

Bring to the boil, and simmer until the mangels are tender. Strain the liquid off and throw out the mangels.

Put the liquid back into the pan with the prepared raisin juice and the orange juice and its rind but having removed the pith and stir in the 3lb. of demerara sugar; bring just to the boil, then take off the heat and strain into a plastic bucket.

When the liquid is lukewarm put in a crushed campden tablet and the pectic enzyme, cover and wait 24 hours, then add yeast and yeast nutrient. Keep the bucket in a warm room all the time, and make sure it is properly covered and the

59

cover is firmly held. Stand for three days but stir daily, then strain into a fermentation demijohn. Fit an airlock, allow to ferment out, rack and clear in the usual way before bottling. Add a little sugar — a tablespoonful or so once or twice — if fermentation seems slow and you think the wine needs feeding. It is ready to drink in six months but you will find it will be much better later.

MARIGOLD WINE

4 quarts marigold flowers
3 lb. granulated sugar.
1 lemon.
1 orange.
½ cup cold strong tea.
6 pts. boiling water.
Campden tablets.
G.P. wine yeast.
Yeast nutrient.

Pick the flowers on a sunny day and wash them well to remove any insects. Place them in a plastic bucket. Grate the rinds of the orange and lemon and squeeze out the juice; add these to the marigold flowers along with the cold tea. Make sure no pith gets in or the wine may acquire a bitter taste.

Pour on the six pints of boiling water and stir well making sure you macerate the flowers. Cover the bucket and leave to stand for four days putting in a crushed campden tablet once the must is cool. Then strain off the liquid into a saucepan and bring it just to the boil. Put the 3 lb. of granulated sugar into another bucket and pour the liquid over this. Stir well until the sugar has dissolved, then leave it to become lukewarm (below 75°F or 24°C).

When the liquid is lukewarm, stir in the yeast and yeast nutrient. Cover the bucket and leave for three days, but stir daily and make sure the room is kept warm. It is now ready to strain into a fermentation demi-john. Fit an airlock and keep in the warm to ferment out. Rack, clear and bottle as usual.

It will be ready to drink in six months.

MARROW WINE

> 4 lb. ripe marrow.
> 3 lb. demerara sugar.
> 1 gallon cold water.
> Prepared juice of ½ lb. raisins.
> Juice of one lemon.
> Campden tablets.
> Pectic enzyme.
> G.P. wine yeast.
> Yeast nutrient.

Prepare your raisin juice as per part 1, 'preparation'.

Take 4 lb. of ripe marrow and remove the pith and seeds but do not peel. Cut it into small pieces and put in a saucepan with the raisin juice and a gallon of cold water. Bring to the boil and simmer until the marrow is tender. Add some more water if it evaporates too much.

Put the 3 lb. of demerara sugar in a plastic bucket and strain the liquid on to it. Add the juice of one lemon. Stir until the sugar has dissolved, and when the liquid is lukewarm, (below 75°F or 24°C) add one crushed campden tablet and the pectic enzyme. Cover and wait 24 hours, then stir in the yeast and yeast nutrient. Always have the bucket positioned in the warm.

Cover the bucket and leave for four days, stirring daily. Strain into a fermentation demi-john and fit an airlock. This wine will need feeding with a tablespoonful or two of sugar every two or three weeks. After about six weeks you may find a thick sediment at the bottom of the demi-john. Siphon the fermenting wine off this into another demi-john, feed with more sugar and re-fit the airlock. Top up if you need to using cold boiled water. After fermentation ceases — more sugar no longer activates the yeast — rack and bottle as usual.

Ready in six months, but much better if you can keep it longer. It is very good!

MULBERRY WINE

4 lb. mulberries.
3 lb. granulated sugar.
6 pts. water.
Pectic enzyme.
Campden tablets.
G.P. wine yeast.
Yeast nutrient.

The mulberries are best picked before they are quite ripe. Wash them and put them into a plastic bucket. Crush the berries with a plastic spoon, then pour over them the six pints of boiling water, add the sugar and stir well.

Cover the bucket and wait till the must is sufficiently cool before putting in a crushed campden tablet and the pectic enzyme. Place in a warm position and cover. After 24 hours you can add the yeast and yeast nutrient. Leave for seven days, stirring daily.

The wine will now be ready to strain into a fermentation

demi-john. Fit an airlock and keep in the warm until fermentation has finished. Then rack into another demi-john and allow to clear before bottling. Never leave the wine on the sediment for more than four weeks as this may affect the taste. Always re-rack (even several times) until the wine is clear enough to bottle.

Keep the wine for at least a year before drinking. The longer you keep it, the better it will be.

ORANGE WINE

4 lb. over-ripe oranges.
3 lb. granulated sugar.
6 pts. of boiling water.
Pectic enzyme.
Campden tablets.
G.P. wine yeast.
Yeast nutrient.

The oranges are best verging towards over-ripe, and a few mouldy ones may be included.

Chop the peel from the oranges and place with the fruit itself into a plastic bucket. Make very sure that no pith gets in, however. Then pour over the six pints of boiling water, add the sugar and stir well. Cover the bucket and leave to cool right down. Add a crushed campden tablet and the pectic enzyme and keep in the warm. After 24 hours add the yeast and yeast nutrient, re-cover and leave for two weeks, stirring it each day.

The wine is then ready to strain into a fermentation demi-john and ferment out through the airlock. After that rack and bottle in the usual way.

Keep the wine for a year before drinking as it will then be

at its best. This really is a lovely wine and very strong. It is a great favourite with many people. Some people prefer it fairly sweet and if necessary a little non-fermenting sweetener will do the trick.

PARSNIP WINE. FIRST METHOD

4 lb. parsnips.
3 lb. granulated sugar.
1 gallon of cold water.
1 lemon
Prepared juice of ½ lb. raisins.
Campden tablets.
Pectic enzyme.
G.P. wine yeast.
Yeast nutrient.

This wine is best made in February or March with parsnips which have remained in the ground all the Winter. Prepare your raisin juice ahead as described in part 1, 'preparation'.

Scrub the parsnips well, but do not peel them; slice them thinly and put them in a large saucepan or preserving pan. Pour in 1 gallon of cold water, or, if you haven't a saucepan big enough, cook 1 lb. of parsnips and ½ of a gallon of water at a time. Cook the parsnips until they are tender, but not mashy. When they are cooked, strain the liquid off.

After straining, throw away the parsnips and return the liquid to the pan. Add the 3 lb. of sugar, the raisin juice and the lemon juice and rind, having removed the pith. Simmer for three-quarters of an hour, stirring occasionally. Strain again into a plastic bucket, and when lukewarm add the pectic enzyme and a crushed campden tablet. Leave covered for 24 hours, placing the bucket in a warm room; then stir in the yeast and yeast nutrient.

Cover the bucket and leave in the warm for four days. Then stir it well and strain into a fermentation demi-john. Fit an airlock and ferment until dry, then rack and clear the wine before bottling. A little feeding with a tablespoonful or two of sugar may be helpful if fermentation seems slow. The wine will be drinkable in six months, but much better if you can leave it longer.

PARSNIP WINE. SECOND METHOD

4 lb. parsnips.
3 lb. demerara sugar.
1 gallon of cold water.
½ oz. hops
Prepared juice of ½ lb. raisins.
1 orange.
1 lemon.
Campden tablets.
Pectic enzyme.
G.P. wine yeast.
Yeast nutrient.

Prepare your raisin juice ahead (see part 1, 'preparation').

Scrub the parsnips well without peeling them and slice thinly into a large saucepan or preserving pan. Pour on 1 gallon of cold water and bring to the boil; simmer until the parsnips are tender but not mashy. Now add ½ oz. of hops and simmer for about half an hour.

Put 3 lb. of demerara sugar into a plastic bucket with the

raisin juice and the chopped peels and the juices from the orange and the lemon but being careful to avoid pith getting in, and strain the liquid on to it. Stir well, and leave until it is lukewarm, pop in a crushed campden tablet and the pectic enzyme, cover and leave for 24 hours in the warm, then add the yeast and yeast nutrient. Cover the bucket and leave it for twelve to fourteen days, stir daily.

Stir into a fermentation demi-john, fit an airlock and place in the warm to ferment until dry. Add a tablespoon or two of demerara sugar at intervals of about two weeks until the wine has finished working.

Rack and allow to clear before bottling.

I think the hops give rather an unpleasant bitter taste when the wine is new, but leave it a year or more and then it's a wonderful wine.

FRESH PEACH WINE

3 lb. peaches.
3 lb. granulated sugar.
6 pts. boiling water.
Pectic enzyme.
Campden tablets.
G.P. wine yeast.
Yeast nutrient.

Choose ripe peaches, wipe them with a damp cloth, cut them in halves and remove the stones. Then put the 3 lb. of peaches in a plastic bucket, pour over the six pints of boiling water, add the sugar and stir them well with a plastic spoon. Cover the bucket and leave till it is lukewarm, then add a crushed campden tablet and the pectic enzyme. Allow 3 days, covered over, stirring daily before putting in the yeast and yeast nutrient, all the time making sure the room the bucket is in is nice and warm. Re-cover and leave alone for one week.

It is now ready to strain into a fermentation demi-john. Fit an airlock and place in the warm to ferment until dry. When the fermentation has finished, rack and allow to clear. Always make sure that your equipment is thoroughly sterilized when racking.

The wine is ready to drink in six months.

DRIED PEACH WINE

2 lb. dried peaches.
3 lb. granulated sugar.
1 gallon of cold water.
Pectic enzyme.
Campden tablets.
G.P. wine yeast.
Yeast nutrient.

Soak 2 lb. of dried peaches for twelve hours in a gallon of cold water. Then place peaches and water in a large saucepan or preserving pan and bring to the boil; simmer for a few minutes, strain the liquid off into a plastic bucket and add 3 lb. granulated sugar. Stir well until the sugar has dissolved. When the liquid is lukewarm stir in the pectic enzyme and a crushed campden tablet, cover and leave in the warm for 24 hours, then put in the yeast and yeast nutrient. Cover the bucket and stand for four days, stirring daily. Remember that the room must be kept warm. Then the wine is ready to strain into a fermentation demi-john to allow fermentation to continue through the airlock. Rack and bottle in the usual way.

The wine should be ready to drink in about nine months.

Don't throw away the peaches after you have strained off the liquid; with some sugar added they will make jam. Put the peaches with a little water in a saucepan and add about four pounds of sugar; then stir over a low heat until the sugar has melted; boil quickly until a little jam dropped on to a cold plate wrinkles when the plate is tilted. Then jar.

PEAR WINE

5 lb. ripe pears.
3 lb. granulated sugar.
1 gallon cold water.
Pectic enzyme.
Campden tablets.
G.P. wine yeast.
Yeast nutrient.

The pears must be very ripe; even the squashy ones will do; this is a good way of using them as pears do go soft so quickly.

Wash the pears or wipe them well with a damp cloth. Do not peel or core them, but cut them in pieces into a large saucepan or preserving pan, and pour on a gallon of cold water. Bring them slowly to the boil, and simmer gently for about half an hour.

Strain the liquid off through the muslin into a plastic bucket, and add the 3 lb. of granulated sugar then stir well to dissolve it and allow to cool right off. Add a crushed campden tablet and the pectic enzyme and leave for 24 hours in the warm; then stir in the yeast and yeast nutrient. Use a plastic spoon for stirring. Cover the bucket keep in warm and stir daily for three days. Then strain into a fermentation demi-john.

Fit an airlock and keep in the warm until fermentation has

ceased. Rack and clear before bottling. Never leave the wine to sit on the sediment for more than four weeks as this may affect the taste. If necessary re-rack several times — i.e. siphon the wine off into another sterile demi-john.

Keep the wine nine months or more before drinking. Store it in a cool dark place if possible. If you prefer a sweeter taste add a little non-fermenting sweetener before drinking.

PLUM WINE

3½ lb. ripe plums.
3 lb. granulated sugar.
6 pts. of boiling water.
Pectic enzyme.
Campden tablets.
G.P. wine yeast.
Yeast nutrient.

Choose really ripe plums; any kind will do. Pick off all stalks and leaves and wash the plums, or wipe them with a damp cloth. Remove the stones, put the plums in a plastic bucket and pour over the six pints of boiling water; stir and mash them with a plastic spoon, adding in the sugar so that it can dissolve, then cover the bucket and leave to cool off. Put in a crushed campden tablet and the pectic enzyme, leave for 24 hours re-covered and then stir in the yeast and yeast nutrient. Cover again and leave for one week, stirring every day and making sure the room is kept warm — around 70°F (20°C).

The wine is then ready to strain into a fermentation demi-john to allow fermentation to continue through an airlock. Rack and bottle in the usual way. The wine should be ready to drink in six months but leave it at least nine months, longer if you can.

POTATO WINE. FIRST METHOD

4 lb. old potatoes.
3 lb. demerara sugar.
1½ gallons cold water.
1 lemon.
1 orange.
Prepared juice of ½ lb.
raisins.
Pinch of ground ginger.
Campden tablets.
Pectic enzyme.
G.P. wine yeast.
Yeast nutrient.

Prepare your raisin juice in advance as described in part 1, 'preparation'.

Wash the potatoes well, but do not peel them. Cut them into small pieces and put into a large saucepan or preserving pan, together with 1½ gallons of cold water. If your pan won't hold this amount, put in as much as you can and add the rest as the water evaporates. Boil the potatoes until they are soft, but not mashy.

Strain off the liquid into a plastic bucket, and add the 3lb. of demerara sugar, the chopped peels and juices but not the pith from the orange and lemon, the raisin juice and the pinch of ground ginger. Stir this well until the sugar has dissolved, then return the liquid to the pan and simmer for half an hour.

Now pour the liquid back into the bucket and wait until it is lukewarm. Then add the pectic enzyme and a crushed campden tablet. Allow 24 hours before stirring in the yeast and yeast nutrient.

Cover the bucket and leave for three days in a nice warm

position. Stir once a day. Strain into a fermentation demi-john, fit an airlock and keep in the warm to ferment in the usual way. Rack and bottle as explained under "basic methods".

Ready in six months.

POTATO WINE. SECOND METHOD

> 3 lb. old potatoes.
> 6 pts. boiling water.
> 3 lb. demerara sugar.
> Prepared juice of 1 lb. raisins.
> ½ oz. hops.
> Campden tablets.
> Pectic enzyme.
> G.P. wine yeast.
> Yeast nutrient.

Wash the potatoes but do not peel them. Cut them into small pieces and put them in a plastic bucket. Add 3 lb. demerara sugar, the prepared juice (see page 18) of the 1 lb. of raisins and the ½ oz. of hops; pour over the six pints of boiling water and stir well with a plastic spoon.

When the contents of the bucket are lukewarm, pop in a crushed campden tablet and the pectic enzyme but cover and wait 24 hours before you stir in the yeast and yeast nutrient. Cover the bucket again, place it in a warm atmosphere and leave for two weeks, stirring daily. After two weeks, strain the liquid off through muslin into a fermentation demi-john. Fit an airlock and keep in the warm to ferment out in the usual way. It is a good tip not to fill the demi-john to the top in case the froth should spill out over the top. Wait until the

71

fermentation has subsided a little before filling to the neck of the demi-john. Rack and clear in the usual way after fermentation is complete. A little feeding is sometimes needed to aid the fermenting process — see under 'using the fermentation demi-john' at the front of the book.

PRUNE WINE

1½ lb. prunes.
3 lb. demerara sugar.
Prepared juice of ½ lb. raisins.
1 gallon cold water.
Pectic enzyme.
Campden tablets.
G.P. wine yeast.
Yeast nutrient.

Wash the prunes remove the stones and put them in a bowl with enough water to cover them and allow for swelling. Soak the prunes for twelve hours, then tip them into a saucepan or preserving pan and add enough water to make it up to a gallon. Prepare the raisin juice (see part 1, 'preparation').

Add the prepared raisin juice to the prunes, then bring them to the boil and simmer for about half an hour. Mash the prunes with a plastic spoon while they are cooking. After half an hour strain off the liquid into a plastic bucket and add the 3 lb. of demerara sugar. Stir until the sugar has dissolved.

When the liquid is lukewarm, add the pectic enzyme and a crushed campden tablet. Wait for 24 hours, leaving the bucket covered, then stir in the yeast and yeast nutrient.

Cover the bucket again and leave it to stand in a warm surrounding for five days, stirring daily. It is then ready to strain into a fermentation demi-john. Fit an airlock and keep in the warm to ferment out in the usual way. The wine is then ready to rack and bottle.

Leave this wine for twelve months before drinking.

QUINCE WINE

3 lb. ripe quinces.
3 lb. granulated sugar.
6 pts. of cold water.
Campden tablets.
G.P. wine yeast.
Yeast nutrient.

Wash the quinces and cut into four, but do not remove the cores as they will improve the flavour of the wine.

Put a crushed campden tablet in the bottom of a plastic bucket and then put the quinces in and pour the six pints of cold water over them. Cover the bucket and leave them to stand for twenty four hours. Make sure the room is warm. Then add yeast and yeast nutrient along with the sugar. Cover and stir well daily for five days.

The wine is then ready to ferment out in the fermentation demi-john. Strain into the demi-john, fit an airlock and keep in the warm in the usual way. Rack after it has fermented to dryness and allow to clear. Do not bottle before the wine is clear. Store the bottles in a cool dark place.

The wine should be ready to drink in nine months, but if you want to keep it longer it will be all the better for it.

RAISIN WINE

3 lb. raisins (large ones).
3 lb. granulated sugar.
6 pts. boiling water.
1 orange.
1 lemon.
Campden tablets.
Pectic enzyme.
G.P. wine yeast.
Yeast nutrient.

Cut up 3 lb. of raisins and put in a plastic bucket with the chopped rind and juice from the orange and lemon being careful not to allow any pith to get in. Pour on the six pints of boiling water, add the sugar and stir well with a plastic spoon. Cover and leave to cool right down. Then add the pectic enzyme and a crushed campden tablet and leave for 24 hours before adding the yeast and yeast nutrient. Have the bucket in a nice warm room all the time. Re-cover when the yeast and yeast nutrient are in and leave for ten days, stirring each day.

Next strain into a fermentation demi-john, fit an airlock and re-place in the warm while the wine ferments to dryness. It is a wine you may need to feed to complete the fermentation and, as explained in the first part of the book, you can add a tablespoonful of sugar every day or two after a while, continuing as required. When the fermentation is finished rack and allow to clear before you bottle. Repeated racking will probably be needed with this wine and you should avoid leaving the wine on top of any large build up of sediment for longer than a few days during the process.

The wine should be ready to drink in six months but it will improve if you leave it longer.

RASPBERRY WINE

> 3½ lb. raspberries.
> 3 lb. granulated sugar.
> 6 pts. of boiling water.
> Campden tablets.
> Pectic enzyme.
> G.P. wine yeast.
> Yeast nutrient.

Pick or buy the raspberries. It does not matter if they are a bit over-ripe, but wash them well to remove any maggots. I find it best to lay them in a bowl of cold water and swish them about gently; if there are many maggots, they float to the top.

Place the raspberries in a plastic bucket and add the sugar and pour over the six pints of boiling water. Stir them well with a plastic spoon while the sugar dissolves. Cover the bucket and leave until it is lukewarm. Then add a crushed campden tablet and the pectic enzyme and leave covered for 24 hours. Then add the yeast and yeast nutrient and leave covered in warm surroundings for ten days. Stir daily.

It will then be ready to strain into a fermentation demi-john, fit an airlock and keep in the warm to ferment to dryness. Rack and bottle in the usual way. It is best if you can put this wine in a dark place as the light could fade the colour. If you can't, then wrap some brown paper around the jar; this will do just as well.

The wine will be ready in six months.

RED CURRANT WINE

3 lb. red currants.
3 lb. granulated sugar.
6 pts. boiling water.
Pectic enzyme.
Campden tablets.
G.P. wine yeast.
Yeast nutrient.

Strip the red currants from the stalks, and put them in a plastic bucket. Pour over the six pints of boiling water, add the sugar and stir well with a plastic spoon. Cover the bucket and leave it to cool off completely. Then add a crushed campden tablet and the pectic enzyme and leave in the warm for 24 hours well covered. Now add the yeast and yeast nutrient and stir well. Leave covered in warm surroundings for seven days, giving the mixture a good stir each day.

After the seven days it is ready to strain into a fermentation demi-john and fit an airlock. Ferment the wine to dryness in the usual way; it is one which may need feeding as explained in part 1. Rack and allow to clear after the fermentation is over and be sure to re-rack if substantial sediment builds up before the wine completely clears. When you have bottled it, keep the wine in a dark place as the colour is liable to fade.

Red currant wine should be ready to drink in nine months, but it will improve immensely if kept longer.

RHUBARB WINE. FIRST METHOD

> 3 lb. rhubarb.
> 3 lb. granulated sugar.
> 6 pts. boiling water.
> Campden tablets.
> Pectic enzyme.
> G.P. wine yeast.
> Yeast nutrient.

Rhubarb wine should be made in May or June. Choose big sticks if possible. It doesn't matter if it is a bit tough.

Wipe your sticks with a damp cloth and cut up into small pieces. Place these in a plastic bucket, add the sugar and pour the six pints of boiling water over. Stir it up well while the sugar dissolves, then cover the bucket and leave to cool down. When lukewarm add the pectic enzyme and a crushed campden tablet and cover. After 24 hours stir in the yeast and yeast nutrient. The mixture needs to ferment in the bucket, helped by a daily stirring, and to be kept in a warm atmosphere and covered, for about seven days before it will be ready to strain into a fermentation demi-john fitted with an airlock for continuation of fermentation to dryness. Rack, allow to clear and bottle as usual.

Rhubarb wine contains oxalic acid and if you discover there is sufficient to affect the taste, making it very sharp, you will need to add some acid reducing solution. Your specialist shop can supply and advise how much to use but use it sparingly as it can remove all the taste of the wine if used to excess.

You can start to drink it after six months.

RHUBARB WINE. SECOND METHOD

3 lb. rhubarb.
3 lb. granulated sugar.
6 pts. cold water.
Campden tablets.
Pectic enzyme.
G.P. wine yeast.
Yeast nutrient.

Some people prefer to make their rhubarb wine by this method. Wipe the sticks with a damp cloth and cut into small pieces; put them into a plastic bucket and pour on the cold water, then stir for a few minutes with a plastic spoon; cover the bucket and leave it alone for ten days in a comfortably warm room.

Next remove any mould which may have formed, most carefully (see Bullace Plum Wine) and then strain off the liquid through muslin into another bucket. Stir in the 3 lb. of granulated sugar thoroughly so you are sure it all dissolves and add a crushed campden tablet and the pectic enzyme. Leave for 24 hours covered over and then stir in the yeast and yeast nutrient. Re-cover, and keep in the warm for four days but this time stir daily. Strain into a fermentation demijohn, fit an airlock and allow to ferment to dryness. Rack, allow to clear and then bottle. As in the first method there is a danger of rhubarb wine being rather sharp (especially from very ripe rhubarb) so an acid reducing agent may be required — (see first method).

This will be ready in six months, but will improve if you keep it longer. Rhubarb wine turns out to be a rather dry wine, very clear and sparkling. It is one of my favourites.

RICE WINE

3 lb. rice.
3 lb. granulated sugar.
6pts warm water
1 lemon.
Prepared juice of 1 lb.
large raisins.
½ cup strong cold tea.
Campden tablets.
G.P. wine yeast.
Yeast nutrient.

Take the prepared raisin juice (see part 1, 'preparation') and place in a plastic bucket with a crushed campden tablet, the 3 lb. of rice and the 3 lb. of granulated sugar. Squeeze the juice from the lemon and add it to these along with the cold tea. Now pour on six pints of warm water and stir well. Wait twenty four hours. Mix the yeast and yeast nutrient with a little lukewarm water (not over 75°F or 24°C) first, so that it can disperse more easily when you stir it in with the other ingredients — which you do next. Stir it in extra well with a plastic spoon. Cover the bucket and stand in a warm place for three days, stirring daily.

Then leave covered for another eight days in a warm atmosphere, without any more stirring.

After this eight days, remove the scum from the top and strain the liquid off into a fermentation demi-john fitted with an airlock.

Place in the warm to ferment to dryness. Rack and clear in the usual way. Rice wine can take a long time to clear, so repeated rackings may be necessary. Rice wine can be very potent, so be careful not to drink too much at a time!

Keep the wine for six months, or longer if you can, before drinking.

SLOE WINE

$3\frac{1}{2}$ lb. sloes.
3 lb. granulated sugar.
6 pts. of cold water.
Pectic enzyme.
Campden tablets.
G.P. wine yeast.
Yeast nutrient.

The sloes are best picked after a frost, usually about the end of September or the beginning of October.

Gather $3\frac{1}{2}$ lb. of sloes and wash them well. Place them in a plastic bucket and pour on the six pints of water. Stir them round for a while, then cover the bucket and leave it to stand in a warm room until a thick mould has formed over the sloes. It may take weeks, or even months, but it doesn't matter how long they stand. The thicker the mould the better the wine.

Lift the mould off carefully without breaking it if possible, then strain off the liquid through muslin into another bucket containing a crushed campden tablet and the pectic enzyme. Leave covered for 24 hours. Then stir in the 3 lb. of granulated sugar, the yeast and yeast nutrient, and cover the bucket. Leave now for five days in the warm, but stir daily. It is then ready to strain into a fermentation demi-john to finish fermenting to dryness. The wine is now ready to rack, allow to clear and bottle in the usual way.

It seems to depend on the time this wine is made as to whether it will turn out sweet enough; I have made two lots within a week of each other and found that one needed sweetening before drinking but the other was quite sweet. So taste it and use a non-fermenting sweetener if you think it needs it. If you are throwing a large gathering it can be quite a job tasting several dozen bottles! I call on some non-drivers to help avoid embarrassment whenever I find myself in this situation.

Remember that all wines lose a certain amount of sweetness as they mature. Worth keeping a year before drinking.

STRAWBERRY WINE

4 lb. ripe strawberries.
3 lb. granulated sugar.
6 pts. of boiling water.
1 lemon.
Pectic enzyme.
Campden tablets.
G.P. wine yeast.
Yeast nutrient.

Use ripe strawberries. It matters not if they are squashy. Remove the hulls and wash the strawberries to get rid of any earth or dust.

Place them in a plastic bucket with the juice of a lemon and the sugar and pour the boiling water over them. With a plastic spoon, mash the strawberries and stir well. Then cover the bucket and leave to cool right down before adding a crushed campden tablet and the pectic enzyme. Re-cover and leave for 24 hours in the warm, then stir in the yeast and yeast nutrient. Cover again and keep in warm surroundings, stirring daily, for one week.

Now it is ready to strain into a fermentation demi-john and fit an airlock. Strain the juice off carefully. Don't squeeze any of the pulp through the muslin. After fermentation is complete — and note that a little feeding may be required as described in part 1 — rack, allow to clear and bottle in the usual way.

This wine will fade if it is not stored in a cool dark place. If this is impossible, wrap a piece of brown paper around the bottles to keep out the light.

Keep at least six months before drinking.

SUGAR BEET WINE

4 lb. sugar beet.
3 lb. granulated sugar.
1 gallon of cold water.
Prepared juice of ½ lb. raisins.
1 lemon.
Campden tablets.
Pectic enzyme.
G.P. wine yeast.
Yeast nutrient.

Prepare your raisin juice in advance as in other recipes (see part 1, 'preparation').

Scrub the sugar beet well, but do not peel. Slice thinly into a large saucepan or preserving pan and add 1 gallon of cold water. If your saucepan won't hold this amount, put some in and add more as the liquid in the pan evaporates.

Bring to the boil and simmer gently until the beet is tender. Then strain the liquid off through muslin into a plastic bucket and throw away the beet. Return the liquid to the pan and add the 3 lb. of sugar, the raisin juice and the chopped peel and juice of the lemon, leaving out any pith. Boil for half an hour then strain off into a bucket and leave covered until lukewarm. Add a crushed campden tablet and the pectic enzyme, re-cover and leave in the warm for 24 hours.

Now stir in the yeast and yeast nutrient, cover the bucket and leave for six days in a nice warm room, stirring daily. Then strain and ferment to dryness in a fermentation demi-john fitted with an airlock. Top up with cold boiled water if the level goes down, as it sometimes will do when wine is fermenting. Rack, allow to clear and bottle in the usual way.

Keep the wine in a cool dark place for at least nine months, when it should be ready to drink.

TEA WINE

4 pints of cold tea.
2 lb. granulated sugar.
Prepared juice of ½ lb. raisins.
2 pts. boiling water.
2 lemons.
Campden tablets.
G.P. wine yeast.
Yeast nutrient.

Follow the instructions in part 1 under 'preparation' to make ready the raisin juice and have to hand the chopped peel and juice of the lemons taking care all the pith is removed. Put all this in a plastic bucket. Dissolve 2 lb. of granulated sugar in two pints of boiling water, pour over the raisins and lemon, stir and pour the four pints of cold tea in. When the mixture has cooled off stir in a crushed campden tablet and cover for 24 hours. Keep in a warm atmosphere and add the yeast and yeast nutrient after this time. Next, cover the bucket and leave it for about three weeks.

After this time you will find a scum on top. Remove this carefully, and strain off the liquid into a fermentation demijohn. Fit an airlock and allow to ferment to dryness. Rack, clear and bottle in the usual way.

Tea wine can be drunk at once, but I think it is best when kept a few months. Keep it in a cool, dark place.

It sounds strange to make wine from tea, but it does turn out a good wine, tasting not in the least like tea. There is no need to make tea especially for this purpose. If you usually throw away half a pot of tea as I think most people do, just save this up until you have four pints. Strain off the tea leaves though!

I suppose the different kinds of tea and the strength of the brew must make some difference to the wine, so yours will probably turn out differently from your neighbours'.

TOMATO WINE

6 lb. ripe tomatoes.
2 lb. granulated sugar.
½ gallon boiling water.
½ teaspoon salt.
Campden tablets.
Pectic enzyme.
G.P. wine yeast.
Yeast nutrient.

Cut up the tomatoes with a stainless steel knife, or one of those little plastic saw-edge knives which do the job so well. Place the cut tomatoes in a piece of muslin and squeeze the juice through into a sterile basin. Pour this over the 2 lb. of granulated sugar in a plastic bucket, add the ½ teaspoon of salt, and pour over half a gallon of boiling water.

Stir well until the sugar has dissolved, allow to cool right down and add a crushed campden tablet and the pectic enzyme. Cover. After 24 hours stir in the yeast and yeast nutrient, re-cover the bucket and leave for three days in a warm place. Strain if necessary and then leave to ferment in a fermentation demi-john. Fit the airlock, place in the warm and allow to ferment to dryness before racking. Allow to clear before bottling. Make sure that the wine is really clear when you bottle, to avoid getting undue sediment in the bottom of the bottle.

Store the bottles in a cool dark place if possible, anyway in the coolest, darkest cupboard you possess.

Keep tomato wine a year or more before you drink it.

TURNIP WINE. FIRST METHOD

4 lb. turnips.
3 lb. granulated sugar.
1 gallon of cold water.
Prepared juice of ½ lb.
raisins.
1 lemon.
1 orange.
Campden tablets.
Pectic enzyme.
G.P. wine yeast.
Yeast nutrient.

Follow part 1, 'preparation' to make the raisin juice ready in advance.

Scrub the turnips well, but do not peel them. Slice thinly into a large saucepan or preserving pan. Pour in 1 gallon of cold water, or as much as the pan will hold. You can add some more as the liquid evaporates in the pan.

Bring to the boil and simmer until the turnips are tender but not mashy. Strain off the liquid into a plastic bucket and throw away the turnips. Put the liquid back in the pan, add the chopped peel and juices of the orange and lemon taking care pith is left out, then the raisin juice and the 3 lb. of sugar. Simmer for another half an hour. Then strain the liquid through muslin into a plastic bucket. When it is lukewarm, add the pectic enzyme and a crushed campden tablet. Leave covered for 24 hours before stirring in the yeast and yeast nutrient. Re-cover and leave in a comfortably warm room for four days, stirring daily. Then strain again if necessary and ferment out in a fermentation demi-john, fitted with an airlock. Make sure that the wine has stopped fermenting before racking. You may need to feed in a tablespoonful or two of sugar to allow the yeast to finish working. Do not add further sugar if there is no reaction to it. See part 1. Allow to clear before bottling.

The wine is ready in six months, but improves greatly with age.

TURNIP WINE. SECOND METHOD

4 lb. turnips.
3 lb. demerara sugar.
1 gallon of cold water.
Prepared juice of ½ lb. raisins.
1 lemon.
1 orange.
½ oz. hops.
Campden tablets.
Pectic enzyme.
G.P. wine yeast.
Yeast nutrient.

Prepare your raisin juice as in first method.

Scrub the turnips, but do not peel them. Slice them thinly into a saucepan or preserving pan and pour on 1 gallon of cold water. Bring to the boil and simmer until the turnips are tender, then add the ½ oz. hops and simmer for another half an hour. I warn you the place will smell like a brewery while these are cooking!

Strain the liquid off through muslin into a plastic bucket and add the sugar the raisin juice and the juice and chopped peel from the lemon and orange (leave out any pith). Stir well until the sugar has dissolved. When the liquid is lukewarm, stir in the pectic enzyme and a crushed campden tablet and cover. After 24 hours stir in yeast and yeast nutrient. Cover again and keep in warm surroundings for ten days. Stir daily.

Then strain into a fermentation demi-john, fit an airlock and allow fermentation to dryness. A little feeding may be needed just as in the first method. Rack, allow to clear and bottle as usual.

The turnips taste very strongly and the hops give the wine a bitter flavour at first, but this wears off and the wine is very good if you can leave it nine months or a year.

WHEAT WHISKY. FIRST METHOD

2 lb. sultanas.
1 pint wheat.
1 lb. barley.
2 large potatoes (finely grated).
1 teaspoon citric acid.
3 lb. demerara sugar.
½ cup cold strong tea.
6 pts. tepid water.
Campden tablets.
G.P. wine yeast.
Yeast nutrient.

Peel the two large potatoes and grate them finely into a plastic bucket. Add the pint of wheat, 1 lb. of barley, 2 lb. of sultanas, citric acid, cold tea and 3 lb. of demerara sugar plus a crushed campden tablet. Pour on six pints of tepid water and stir well until the sugar has dissolved. Make sure the must cools to below 75°F (or 24°C) and, unless package instructions declare that you should wait 24 hours, then add the yeast and yeast nutrient and stir again.

Cover the bucket and leave for at least ten days but preferably up to three weeks. Stir daily and make sure the room always remains warm. Then strain the liquid off into a fermentation demi-john. Fit an airlock and keep in the warm to ferment to dryness. If fermentation seems a bit slow, feed with a couple of tablespoonfuls of sugar to help things along, every day or two. Once no fizzy reaction occurs as you put the sugar in, you know fermentation is complete. Then rack and leave while it clears but do not leave the wine on its sediment for longer than four weeks without re-racking. This is a difficult wine to clear, so you may have to rack several times before you can bottle.

Leave the wine for at least nine months — much longer if you can — as this is a wine that improves immensely with age. It becomes very much like whisky as it matures.

WHEAT WHISKY. SECOND METHOD

1 pint of wheat.
2 lb. sultanas.
2 large potatoes (finely grated).
3 lb. demerara sugar.
Grated rind and juice of
two lemons.
$\frac{1}{2}$ cup cold tea.
6 pts. tepid water.
Campden tablets.
Pectic enzyme.
G.P. wine yeast.
Yeast nutrient.

Peel and grate the potatoes. Mix into a plastic bucket along with the pint of wheat, 2 lb. of sultanas, 3 lb. of demerara sugar, the grated rind and juice of two lemons (no pith), the cold tea, the pectic enzyme and a crushed campden tablet.

Pour on six pints of tepid water and mix very thoroughly with a plastic spoon. Leave covered for 24 hours then stir in the yeast and yeast nutrient. Cover the bucket and stand for ten to fourteen days in the warm, stirring daily.

You are now ready to strain off the wine carefully and ferment out in a fermentation demi-john. Fit an airlock, place in the warm and allow fermentation to continue until it has finished. Rack and leave to clear before bottling as usual.

You may need to feed during fermentation as in the first method.

Likewise you may need to rack several times.

Keep for six months or longer.

WHEAT WINE

1½ lb. wheat.
3 lb. granulated sugar.
1 gallon of cold water.
Prepared juice of ½ lb. raisins.
1 lemon.
1 orange.
½ teaspoon ground ginger.
½ cup cold strong tea.
Campden tablets.
Pectic enzyme.
G.P. wine yeast.
Yeast nutrient.

Follow the instructions in part 1, 'preparation' to make your raisin juice in advance.

Put the 1½ lb. of wheat in a large saucepan or preserving pan with 1 gallon of cold water and bring to the boil. Simmer for half an hour, then strain the liquid into a plastic bucket. Add 3 lb. of granulated sugar, the chopped peels and juices of the fruit (no pith), the raisin juice and ½ teaspoon of ground ginger. Pour in the cold tea and stir well with a plastic spoon.

When the mixture is lukewarm, add the pectic enzyme and a crushed campden tablet. Leave covered for 24 hours in the warm and stir in the yeast and yeast nutrient. Cover the bucket and leave it for ten days, stirring occasionally and always watching that the room remains comfortably warm; then strain into a fermentation demi-john. Fit an airlock and keep in the warm to ferment until dry; sometimes feeding will be necessary to help the process as in the other wheat recipes. Rack into another demi-john and clear the wine before bottling. Again, this wine may need several rackings before it clears but be patient, it is worth it in the end.

Keep the wine at least six months, and much longer if possible.

PART IV
OTHER DRINKS

GINGER BEER

To make one ginger beer plant and your first 16 pints of ginger beer:

Start with:
1 level tablespoonful ground ginger.
1 level tablespoonful granulated sugar.
2 oz. baker's yeast.
1 pint water.

Additional plant food:
Ground ginger approx 1 oz.
Granulated sugar approx. 3 oz.

Plus, per 16 pints of ginger beer:
Juice of 6-8 lemons.
2 lb. granulated sugar.
Water to top up.

By far the best way to make ginger beer is by cultivating a ginger beer plant. You always need to make lots and lots when there are children around and with a plant you can carry on ad infinitum!

Put the yeast into a sterile open glass jar big enough to

hold rather more than a pint. Pour in the pint of water and follow with the level tablespoonfuls of ginger and sugar. Cover with clean linen. Beginning the next day feed in once a day equal amounts of ginger and sugar, about one heaped teaspoonful of each. By the middle of the second week the base liquid for your 16 pints of ginger beer will be ready to syphon off.

Keep the sediment if you want to go on making more and more ginger beer because you can divide and multiply! Divide the plant into two glass jars, pour a pint of water into each, then add ginger and sugar as before for the next week and a half, etc., etc.

To turn your base liquid into 16 pints ginger beer, dissolve 2 lb. sugar into 2 pints boiling water and add the juice of the lemons (if you warm them first more juice will be extracted). Pour this liquid into a 2 gallon sterilised plastic bucket, add 1 gallon cold water and stir well. Now stir in the previously syphoned off base liquid. Top up with cold water until you have 2 gallons and stir the whole mixture thoroughly.

The mixture can now be poured into its final bottles where it needs to stand at room temperature preferably for several hours before corking. There is no need to jam the corks down, indeed if the ginger beer turns out more lively than you expect with these rough and ready measures it is better for the cork to pop out than for the bottle to burst! On this account it is important to allow a minimum air space below the cork of 2½" — 3" when you have corked it and to use strong bottles such as the beer, lemonade or cider types.

You may experience a 'temperamental' brew which blows the corks off and fizzes over more than usual. The liveliness of different brews from the same recipe can vary quite widely depending on atmospheric conditions, etc. It is therefore necessary to keep a fairly constant eye on your bottles so that you can promptly re-cork any which blow. To avoid losing your ginger beer through frothing over, (and the trouble is once a cork blows and the brew fizzes over, you lose it!) an alternative is to use a safety cork obtainable from your home-winemaking specialist shop.

After corking it will be a grand drink in about two weeks.

MEAD

3 lb. honey.
2 whites of eggs.
G.P. wine yeast.
Yeast nutrient.
1 lemon.
1½ gallons of cold water.

Put the 3 lb. of honey and grated rind of the lemon in a large saucepan or preserving pan, with one and a half gallons of cold water. Beat the whites of the two eggs until they are frothy and add to the rest of the ingredients.

Place the pan over the heat and stir as the mixture comes to the boil. Then simmer gently for one hour. Pour the liquid into a plastic bucket and leave it to become lukewarm, then stir in the yeast and yeast nutrient.

Cover the bucket and leave in a fairly warm place for three days; stir daily. Then strain through muslin and ferment in a fermentation demi-john with an airlock. Ferment, rack and bottle as you would a wine.

Store the bottles in a cool, dark place, and keep the mead at least a year before drinking it, as it improves immensely with keeping.

Not many people drink mead now, but it was a very popular drink in olden times.

CIDER

For the best cider, a mixture of different varieties of apples is best. Those usually chosen are non-keepers, small sour or windfalls, with, if desired, a few crab-apples. An odd rotten apple in a large number is permissible, but otherwise they should be sound.

Before the Second World War, my historical searches tell me there were travelling cider presses in some districts, as many farms and cottages had a small orchard. This practice seems to have disappeared, though it may still exist in a few country areas.

To get your apples pressed ideally, a cider factory is the thing, if you can persuade them to do it. Alternatively, a cider factory might sell you the newly pressed apply juice. For those who cannot find a cider factory, you can buy a fruit press from your local specialist shop.

The juice should be put into a wooden cask — a 30-gallon ex-brandy cask is ideal for first-class good keeping cider. Base your calculations on the fact that a ton of apples makes approximately 150 gallons of cider, therefore a cwt. makes approximately $7\frac{1}{2}$ gallons. Any good size wooden or plastic cask is suitable but the larger the better as fermentation goes on longer in a greater quantity of juice, thus producing a high alcohol content. The cask should stand in a cool place either on its side or end, wherever the bung hole is uppermost.

Never bung up the hole while fermentation is still going on; unless to bring the cask home, perhaps! After about forty-eight hours the apple juice will start to ferment and white froth will bubble up through the bung hole. This will continue for about three weeks. When fermentation has almost stopped, some juice should be siphoned out of the cask with a short length of sterile clear plastic pipe. The amount of juice removed should be sufficient to dissolve the required quantity of sugar.

Add 2 to 4 lb. of sugar (depending on how sweet you want

the cider) per gallon *in the cask* to the juice you have removed, and dissolve over heat. When quite dissolved, allow to cool, then return to the cask. Owing to the addition of the sugar all the sweetened juice will not go back in at once. During fermentation, which will go on for about two weeks, the quantity of liquid in the cask reduces so that you can add the surplus gradually (as space permits). When fermentation has nearly finished, if all the 'juice and sugar mixture' is not in the cask, siphon out enough juice to allow this to go in. Bottle what you take out and use to keep the cask full while the cider is maturing — as the quantity reduces during this process. Developing airspace in the cask will otherwise allow bacilli to breed and turn the cider acid.

When the juice has completely ceased to 'bubble up' bung the cask up tightly with either cork or wood, and leave for eight months.

Cider is usually made in October-November, and should be left *as long as possible* — up to two years before opening it, but at least until the cuckoo sings the following year. Then the cask may be tapped, or the cider bottled down with care.

Innocent to taste but powerful — up to 15% alcohol can be achieved.

BEER

3 lb. Malt Extract.
2 oz. hops.
1 lb. granulated sugar.
Top fermenting Beer
    Yeast.
4 gallons of water.

This recipe makes four gallons of normal strength beer. If you wish to brew something stronger, cut down the amount of water. If you would like it weaker, then increase the amount of water.

To make half the quantity, halve the ingredients exactly, and, in the same way, if doubling the quantity, see that you double all the ingredients and do not forget any.

To make four gallons, you will need a plastic bucket to hold five gallons. You can make whatever quantity you wish in this bucket, provided that you do not wish to make more than 5 gallons.

Put the hops into a large pot and add 4 pints of cold water. Cover and boil vigorously for 30 minutes. Keep a pinch of hops out to add during the last five minutes of boiling. Meanwhile, put the container of malt extract in hot water to make it run easily and then pour the malt into the 5-gallon bucket which you have sterilized.

Sterilization is important. To rinse with boiling water is not good enough. Buy from your chemist or specialist shop 4 oz. of sodium meta-bisulphite and some citric acid. Dissolve the sodium meta-bisulphite in the quantity directed on the package with one teaspoon of citric acid in one quart of water and rinse out the bucket with this solution. If you keep the solution in a corked or screw-top bottle, you can use it several times.

Strain the boiling hops over the malt extract, add the sugar and stir until dissolved. Make up the quantity required with cold water, stirring well. When the liquid is cool to the touch, approx. 65°F-70°F, stir in the yeast. Place the bucket in a warm area and cover with a tea-towel.

After two days, a deep froth will appear. This froth will be speckled with dark brown, dead yeast. Remove this froth with a plastic strainer. Do not use metal unless it is stainless steel. The fermentation will continue for 4-6 days. When the fermentation is nearly finished, it is time to siphon into beer bottles.

You can normally tell this when the froth which has covered the top of the beer reduces in size to a ring of about 2 inches diameter, in the centre. A surer way of determining the bottling stage is by use of the hydrometer. Float the hydrometer in the beer, and bottle when it reads 1005. Do not bottle if the reading is over 1010.

A word about bottles. It is advisable to use either beer or cider bottles. The pressure of gas in the beer is sufficient to burst bottles not made for the purpose. You can buy specially designed plastic pressure barrels to dispense your beer. These save a great deal of work washing, sterilizing and filling bottles, and you can pour out a lovely clear pint at will.

If you use bottles, sterilize them with your solution of sodium meta-bisulphite and citric acid, prime the beer by adding $\frac{1}{2}$ level teaspoon of sugar to each pint bottle, and fill to within 1 inch of the top. Stopper the bottles with either crown corks or screw caps and place them in the warm to ferment for two days. After this period, it is better to put the bottles in a cool place. This will speed up the clearing process which should not take more than one week. Finings can be used, but they should not be necessary. The beer can be drunk after two weeks, but it improves if you can keep it another two weeks.

If you are using a pressure barrel, prime the beer by adding $\frac{1}{2}$ oz. of sugar per gallon of beer into the barrel. Place the barrel in a warm place for two days to re-ferment. Loosen the screw cap during this period to allow the gas to escape. After two days, screw the cap down tight and remove the barrel to a cool place to clear. The beer takes longer to clear in the barrel — about two or three weeks, but is all the better for the waiting.

CHRISTMAS DRINKS

At Christmas the drinks seem to disappear like magic. What with parties, odd callers and extra drinks for the family one needs to spend a fortune to keep up with the demand. Unless, of course, one has home-made wine to fall back on.

But I admit, to offer a visitor a glass of home-made wine at the festive season may seem rather tame, so I dress up my drinks a little. I have found that with a little experimenting I can make quite a good wine cocktail with my own wine. I will write out one or two to give you an example, but it only needs a little mixing and tasting to improvise a drink with what you have at hand.

LUCKY DIP

The first one I call 'Lucky Dip'.
$\frac{1}{2}$ bottle of rhubarb wine.
$\frac{1}{2}$ bottle of marrow wine.
1 wineglass of ginger wine.
1 wineglass of whisky.
1 wineglass of rum.
1 tumbler of carrot wine.
1 tumbler of ginger beer.

Just mix them all together; it sounds a strange mixture, but tastes good.

'GUESS WHAT'

$\frac{1}{2}$ bottle blackberry wine.
$\frac{1}{2}$ bottle rhubarb wine.
1 wineglass ginger wine.
1 wineglass port wine.
$\frac{1}{2}$ wineglass whisky.

Mix together and you have the answer!

100

ORANGE COCKTAIL

1 bottle orange wine.
1 wineglass whisky.
Dash of rum.

If you prefer brandy or gin as the spirit content just experiment a little using these; of course you can be more extravagant with the spirits if you wish, but as a general party drink I find those I have mentioned quite adequate.

If you have a favourite punch recipe, which needs a bottle of sherry or other wine, substitute a bottle of home-made wine or use half and half.

I had a bottle of beetroot wine which was not really old enough to drink, but I wanted a red wine, so I poured a glass of port into the decanter and poured the beet wine on to it. The flavour was improved and several people praised the wine.

My marrow wine, although quite strong already, I thought could do with a fillip for the party season. So to one bottle I added a glass of whisky and to another a glass of rum and corked them down till required. One visitor after having two glasses of the rum marrow wine said he felt quite tipsy on going out into the air and was jolly all the way home.

So, if like me you have to economise at times remember these tips. It requires little spirits or port and it is so much nicer to be able to serve out drinks with a liberal hand, instead of with one eye on the bottle all the time.

BLACKBERRY CORDIAL

2 quarts blackberries.
1/4 pint cold water.
1 lb. granulated sugar.
   to each quart of
   juice.
8 cloves.
1/2 nutmeg.
Wineglass of rum or
   brandy.

Wash the blackberries and put them in a thick saucepan with a quarter of a pint of water; simmer very gently until the fruit is mashy. Tip the blackberries into a piece of muslin and squeeze all the juice out into a bowl. Measure the juice, and for each quart allow a pound of granulated sugar.

Put the juice and sugar into the saucepan and add the eight cloves and half a nutmeg, not grated. Boil for half an hour stirring all the time. Skim off any scum that forms.

Take the saucepan off the heat and add the wineglass of rum or brandy. Let the cordial cool a little, then pour into warm bottles, put the corks in tightly and, to make sure the cordial will keep, seal the bottles with wax.

This is a very good drink for preventing or curing colds and chills — take a wineglass when necessary.

FRUIT SYRUPS. 7 RECIPES

GENERAL HINTS

Fruit syrups make a good base for many summer drinks, or, with those such as black currant, excellent winter hot drinks for sore throats and colds. These can be made as the various fruits become available and stored in the same way as bottled fruit.

It is best to use the juicy fruits, as it is unnecessary to add water. Any less juicy fruits require a little water added and boiling to extract the juice.

To make certain the fruit syrups will keep, it is best to sterilize them by the water immersion method, as in bottling fruit. Pour the syrup into a preserving jug, screw on the metal top, then give a half turn back to loosen it. Place this in a saucepan of cold water with a folded cloth underneath and bring slowly to the boil. Boil for about twenty minutes, then remove carefully and stand on a wooden surface or dry folded cloth. Screw the top on tightly and leave to cool.

The syrup will retain its colour and flavour better if it is stored in a dark place. It should keep indefinitely. Once the jar is opened, use it up before it attracts mould.

BLACKBERRY SYRUP

3 pints blackberry juice.
3 lb. granulated sugar.
2 pints water.

Pick really ripe blackberries. Look them over, remove any stems or hulls and then wash them well.

Place in a saucepan with just enough water to prevent burning — about half a teacup to a pound of fruit. Simmer very gently for twenty minutes. Remove from the heat and mash the berries with a wooden spoon. Strain the juice off through muslin into a jug.

Allow three pounds of granulated sugar and two pints of water to every three pints of blackberry juice. Put the sugar and water in a saucepan and bring slowly to the boil; remove any scum; boil for five minutes; then add the blackberry juice and boil for another five minutes. Remove from the heat and allow to cool before bottling. If you intend to use it in a few days it will keep in bottles, but if it is to be kept for some time then it is better to sterilize it (as was shown under general hints at the start of this section), otherwise a mould would probably form in the bottle.

Store the syrup in a cool, dark place. This syrup is also a great preventive for colds and chills if used as a base for a hot drink.

BLACKCURRANT SYRUP

3 pints blackcurrant juice.
3 lb. granulated sugar.
2 pints water.

Pick the blackcurrants when ripe. Remove the stalks and wash the currants well. Put them in a bowl and mash with a wooden spoon. Add some boiling water, about half a teacup to 2 lb. of fruit. Mash them again. Then strain the juice off through muslin.

Measure the juice into a jug. For every three pints of juice allow 3 lb. of granulated sugar, and two pints of water. Put the sugar and water in a saucepan and bring it slowly to the boil, skim off any scum that rises. Boil for five minutes, then add the blackcurrant juice and boil for another ten minutes. Remove from the heat and allow to cool before bottling. Pour it into bottles and seal if you only intend to keep it for a short time. But if you wish to keep it for some months, then it is best to sterilize it in the same way as for bottled fruit, (see page 103.) Store it in a dark place.

This syrup is very good for winter coughs and colds; just dilute it to taste in hot or cold water. Also, of course, it contains Vitamin C, which is so necessary to good health, especially for children.

GINGER SYRUP

4 oz. root ginger.
2 pints water.
1 lemon.
1 lb. of granulated sugar
  to every pint of liquid.

Bruise the ginger well — I always break mine into small pieces — and put it with two pints of water in a saucepan. Add two or three thin strips of the yellow rind of the lemon. Boil gently for about three quarters of an hour, then strain through muslin into a jug.

For every pint of liquid allow 1 lb. of granulated sugar. Put all this into a saucepan and add the juice of the lemon. Boil for fifteen minutes, removing the scum as it rises. Leave it to cool, then strain and bottle.

Seal the bottles well, or if you intend to keep the syrup for some time, pour it into preserving jars and sterilize it, as explained a few pages back. This will then keep for years if it is stored in a cool, dark place.

It is a very useful syrup on cold winter days; a little added to a glass of hot water will make a warming drink. It can also be used to flavour cakes and puddings.

LEMON SYRUP

> Enough lemons to yield
> 1 pint of lemon juice.
> Grated rind from 3 of the lemons.
> 3 lb. granulated sugar.
> 2 pints of water.

Wash the lemons and grate the rind from them. Squeeze the juice out until you have a pint of juice. If the lemons are warmed first, much more juice can be extracted. Put the grated rind and 3 lb. of granulated sugar in a saucepan with two pints of water. Gradually bring this to the boil, stirring all the time, and boil for ten minutes. Skim if necessary. Pour in the pint of lemon juice and boil for another ten minutes.

Remove the scum, strain the syrup through muslin and leave to cool. When cool pour it into bottles and seal well, or put in preserving jars and sterilize, as explained for earlier syrup recipes. Keep the bottles in a cool, dark place.

You may wish to make only half this quantity. If you do, be sure to halve the amounts exactly; it is quite easy to forget some of the ingredients, and, of course, this will put the whole recipe out of balance.

ORANGE SYRUP

> Enough oranges to yield
>   1 pint orange juice.
> Grated rind of 3
>   oranges.
> Grated rind of 1
>   lemon.
> 2 pints of water.
> 3 lb. granulated sugar.

Wash the oranges and lemon; grate the rind from the oranges and lemon. Try not to let any pith through your grater. Squeeze the juice from the oranges until you have a pint. Add the juice of the lemon. Mix the grated rind and the juice together.

Put the 3 lb. of granulated sugar in a thick saucepan with two pints of cold water and bring it slowly to the boil. Boil for five minutes, skimming off any scum that forms. Then add the pint of orange, lemon juice and grated rind, and boil for another fifteen minutes, still removing any scum.

Strain the syrup and, when cool, pour into bottles and seal well. If you intend to keep the syrup for any length of time, it is best to sterilize it in preserving jars. (See earlier syrup recipes).

Keep the bottles in a cool, dark place. They will keep for years if sterilized properly. Once a bottle has been opened, however, it must be used fairly quickly.

RASPBERRY SYRUP

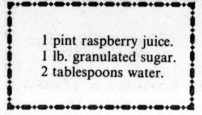

1 pint raspberry juice.
1 lb. granulated sugar.
2 tablespoons water.

Choose nice ripe raspberries and wash them carefully to remove any maggots. Be careful not to lose too much juice while doing this.

Place the raspberries in a saucepan with a thick bottom, with two tablespoons of cold water. Simmer very, very gently until the raspberries are mashy and the juice runs out. Remove them from the heat and mash the berries thoroughly with a wooden spoon. Strain through muslin and measure the liquid into a jug.

For each pint of raspberry juice allow one pound of granulated sugar. Return the juice to the saucepan with the sugar and bring to the boil. Boil for ten minutes. Remove the scum, strain, and while still hot, pour into hot bottles and seal.

If you intend to keep the syrup for some time it is safer to pour into preserving jars and sterilize as explained for other syrups.

Keep the bottles in a cool, dark place.

STRAWBERRY SYRUP

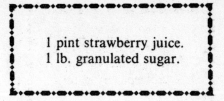

1 pint strawberry juice.
1 lb. granulated sugar.

Pick or buy ripe strawberries, but don't use any bruised ones. Remove the hulls and wash the strawberries, then pack them into large preserving jars and stand these in a saucepan of cold water. Place a folded cloth underneath to prevent the jars from cracking, and bring slowly to the boil. Do not screw the jars down. Boil them until the juice begins to run out. This will not take long.

Remove the jars, remembering to stand them on a wooden surface or folded cloth, or the jars will crack. Mash the fruit to extract the remaining juice. Then strain it all through muslin.

Put the strawberry juice in a saucepan. For each pint of juice add 1 lb. of granulated sugar. Bring slowly to the boil and boil for fifteen minutes, stirring well all the time. Remove the scum, strain into a bowl and leave until cold. Then pour into preserving jars and sterilize, as for other syrups. If you intend to use it fairly soon, pour it into bottles and seal the tops.

Keep it in a dark place if possible. It is used for summer drinks with water added.

PART V

CHILDREN'S DRINKS, TEAS
AND COFFEES

It is often a problem to know what to give children to drink in Summer. One can buy endless varieties of beverages but they are mostly expensive. I do not think the cheap ones of the gassy type are very good.

I have collected a few recipes, some of which, if they are a little extravagant, are more wholesome than the manufactured variety. The others are economical and excellent thirst quenchers.

Children appreciate a drink much more if it is made to look attractive. When sometimes I have had only one orange or lemon left, with a little ingenuity I have made it up into some sort of drink, and the children have thought it marvellous because it was pretty.

Milk can be made attractive in the same way. My daughters will not drink plain milk at home. They used to force it down somehow at school. I think that it is mainly because it looks so dull. Very often I have added a little cochineal and sugar, called it by some exotic name, and it has been swallowed to the last drop; yet the only flavouring was sugar.

I think it especially inviting on a summer day to see a tall glass jug of lemonade, with cool-looking slices of lemon or cucumber floating on top. The floating pieces seem to give it an added charm. I think they have a cooling effect, in the same way as fish swimming in a tank are soothing to watch.

Hot drinks also can be made more appealing by a little deception. My children don't like cocoa made in the usual way — mixed in a cup and hot water poured on — but if I boil it in a saucepan until it is frothy and then call it hot

111

chocolate, they love it. I hope they do not read this, as they will be annoyed to think I have deceived them! It is not the proper thing to do, according to child psychologists. Still, chocolate is made from cocoa, so perhaps I am right after all.

At party times I always mix a fruit cocktail for the children so that they do not feel left out of things while the adults are quaffing wine. It is not much trouble and I like any excuse to concoct a new drink.

I have labelled the following drinks as 'children's drinks', but they need not be confined to children. My husband and I enjoy them, too. In fact, these were recipes where they were all willing to act as guinea-pigs!

CHOCOLATE MILK WHIP

2 oz. plain or milk chocolate.
½ pint fresh milk.
Some cream or ice-cream.

This can be made as a hot or cold drink. To make a hot drink put the 2 oz. of chocolate in a pudding basin and stand it in a pan of hot water. Melt it slowly and gradually beat in with a fork the half pint of fresh milk. When the milk is thoroughly beaten in, remove the pan from the heat and using an eggbeater or rotary whisk, beat until the mixture is frothy. Pour it into a glass and add a spoonful of cream; do not stir this in.

To make a cold drink, melt the chocolate in the same way, but only beat in a quarter pint of milk. Take the basin out of the saucepan and beat in the rest of the cold milk. Chill

112

thoroughly, then whisk until frothy. Add a spoonful of ice-cream to the glass. Both these recipes can have sugar added to taste. These make very nourishing drinks for invalids or children who will not drink plain milk. I have only given amounts for one glassful, so the ingredients can be increased in proportion to the number of glasses required.

CHILDREN'S PARTY SPECIAL

1 Tin pineapple juice.
1 Glass of lemon squash.
1 pint of cold water.
1 bottle 'fizzy' lemonade.
A few glacé or maras-
    chino cherries.
Sprigs of mint.
Borage leaves.
1 lemon.

Empty the pineapple juice into a large glass bowl or jug. Add the glass of lemon squash and the pint of cold water and stir well. Pour in a bottle of 'fizzy' lemonade — it can be coloured if preferred and will make the drink look gayer. Slice the lemon very thinly and add it; stir the concoction very gently to mix it well. Add the cherries, maraschino or glacé, whichever you have handy, and some sprigs of mint and borage leaves. If preferred, pineapple pieces can also be added to make it more exciting. Remember to provide spoons as well as drinking straws.

For older children the recipe can be altered a little. Squeeze the juice out of the lemon instead of slicing it, and leave out the mint and borage leaves. Serve the drink in small glasses with a cherry on a stick in each.

ECONOMICAL LEMONADE

> 3-4 lemons.
> ½ lb. granulated sugar.
> ½ oz. cream of tartar.
> 2 quarts of boiling water.
> Sprigs of mint.

This is a good cheap lemonade for those with large, thirsty families. It is very refreshing on a hot, sticky day.

Wash the lemons and slice them thinly, place in a jug with ½ lb. of granulated sugar and ½oz. cream of tartar. Pour over this the two quarts of boiling water and stir well with a wooden spoon. Cover the jug and leave it to cool. Preferably, leave it overnight.

Pour the lemonade into glass jugs and leave the slices of lemon floating on top. Wash a few sprigs of mint and add these to the jugs. Make sure the lemonade is really cold before drinking. If possible, leave in a refrigerator for a while.

This is a good drink for children's parties or picnics. In the summer, my children often asked to have their tea packed to take in the fields, and they liked a large bottle of lemonade each, and often one for their friends. Under these conditions, one bought bottle is no good at all, unless you are feeling rich and can provide a bottle for each! My children usually got the home-made variety.

KIDDIES KOKTAIL

$\frac{1}{2}$ pint of any fruit juice.
Tumbler of non-alcoholic
  ginger wine.
$\frac{1}{2}$ pint coloured
  lemonade.
Some maraschino
  cherries.

Any fruit juice will do; that strained off stewed fruit, the juice from a tin of fruit, or fresh fruit juice. Fruit syrups mixed with a little water are very good to use.

Put the juice in a jug and pour on the tumbler of non-alcoholic ginger wine, add half a pint of coloured lemonade, matched up to the fruit juice. I find that red is the most popular colour. Mix it all thoroughly. Serve up in small glasses and — to make the children feel quite grown-up — put a cherry on a stick into each glass.

My children insist that the type of glass makes the drink taste different — how true — and they will cheerfully fill a small glass many times rather than save their energy and have one large glass. My youngest daughter even appropriated a small empty champagne bottle, into which she carefully poured her's before transferring it to a glass. To me it seems wasted energy, but perhaps my imagination is not so good!

LEMON BARLEY

> 2 oz. pearl barley.
> 1½ pints of cold water.
> 1 lemon.
> 2 tablespoons sugar.

Put the pearl barley in a saucepan with the 1½ pints of cold water and one or two pieces of lemon peel and simmer for about an hour. Pearl barley seems an awkward kind of thing to cook, and the first time I made this drink I found that if I put the lid on, the water boiled over. I left the lid off and forgot it for more than an hour and found the pearl barley had caked in a hard mass on the bottom of the saucepan. So now I compromise. I put the lid half on, and if the liquid seems to be getting dangerously low, I add a little more water. Do remember to simmer very gently.

Strain the barley water into a jug and stir in two tablespoons of sugar and the juice of a lemon. Leave it to cool. Dilute to taste and, if necessary, add some more sugar; it depends whether you have a very sweet tooth.

Do not keep the lemon barley for more than a few days. You may of course use orange juice for flavouring. This is a good beverage for invalids and children, as barley is nourishing and good for the body internally.

MARROW CREAM

1 Ripe marrow.
1 lb. granulated sugar.
1 lemon.
1 pint of warm water.
½ oz. of baker's yeast acting or
  quick acting G.P. yeast.

Cut up about 2 lb. of ripe marrow into very small cubes, omitting the rind and pith. Put the cubes in a bowl and pour over 1 lb. of granulated sugar so that the marrow is completely covered. Cover the bowl and leave it overnight.

In the morning you will find that the sugar has dissolved in the marrow juice; pour this off into a jug. Now pour a pint of warm water over the remaining marrow cubes, stir together for a few minutes, then pour off the mixture into the marrow juice.

Add the juice of the lemon and stir in ½ oz. of yeast. Cover the bowl and leave it in a fairly warm place for several hours when you will find it has become frothy. Stir again and it is then ready to drink.

It is best drunk while fresh, as if you keep it for more than a day or two, it will begin to turn into wine. This is quite a health-giving drink, as both the yeast and lemon contain vitamins and the sugar provides energy.

ORANGE AND LEMON COCKTAIL

> 2 oranges.
> 1 lemon.
> $1\frac{1}{4}$ pints of cold water.
> $\frac{1}{4}$ pint of hot water.
> Sugar to taste.
> Sprig of mint.
> Sprig of borage.
> Slices of cucumber.

Cut the oranges in half, and squeeze the juice from one and a half oranges. Cut the lemon in half and squeeze the juice from one half. Cut the two remaining halves of orange and lemon into thin slices and put them in a jug with the juice. Add some sugar — two or three tablespoons according to taste. Pour on a quarter pint of hot water and stir well until the sugar has dissolved. Then gradually add the $1\frac{1}{4}$ pints of cold water.

Float a few sprigs of mint and borage leaves on top, and slide some long strips of cucumber peel down the sides of the jug. Use a glass jug. Chill thoroughly before serving. If your refrigerator is crowded, stand the jug in a bowl of cold water and cover with a damp cloth. Stand the bowl on the floor in a draught.

The mint and borage give the drink an unusual flavour, very summery and refreshing. The children think it is a lovely drink, and it looks attractive with the cucumber, the orange and lemon slices and mint sprigs floating on top.

POPPETS' PUNCH

½ pint of any fruit juice
  from stewed fruit or
  fruit syrup made up
  to half a pint with
  water.
1 Bottle of lemonade.
Some maraschino
  cherries.
Ice-cream.
Tinned fruit.

The fruit juice can be any strained off stewed fruit; see that there are no bits floating. Alternatively, make up some fruit syrup to half a pint by adding water. (See syrup recipes earlier.)

Put the half a pint of fruit juice in a quart jug and pour on a bottle of lemonade. Match up the colour and flavour of the fruit juice with one of the proprietary brands of 'fizzy' drinks or use plain bottled lemonade. Mix well. Drop a few maraschino cherries or glacé cherries into the mixture. Add a spoonful of ice-cream to each glass and don't forget to perch a cherry on each one.

To make this more of a party drink, make double the quantity and put it in a large glass bowl. Float pieces of tinned fruit in this, such as pineapple or peaches. Serve up with a ladle and add a spoonful of ice-cream to each glass. Provide each glass with a long spoon and drinking straw.

For a winter party, try leaving out the ice-cream. However, children enjoy ice-cream whatever the weather!

STRAWBERRY MILK SHAKE

½ lb. of strawberries.
1 pint of fresh milk.
2 tablespoons of ice-cream.
1 tablespoon of caster sugar or glucose.

Wash the strawberries and pick out two of the best looking and put to one side. Lay a piece of muslin in a pudding basin and place the rest of the strawberries in this. Mash them well with a wooden spoon, then lift the corners of the muslin and squeeze the juice and as much of the pulp as possible through into the basin.

Sprinkle on to this a tablespoon of caster sugar — or if you wish it to be more energizing, a heaped tablespoon of glucose; this does not sweeten as much as sugar. Beat this in with a fork and gradually add the fresh milk. Then use a whisk and whisk until it is frothy.

Pour this into two tall glasses. Add a tablespoon of ice-cream and perch a strawberry on top. Provide a long spoon and a straw. If the drink is not very pink, add a few drops of cochineal while whisking.

If you grow strawberries, this is not an expensive drink, and it is one way of getting children to drink milk. I find that when milk is coloured and sweetened, children are more eager to drink it.

ORANGE REFRESHER

1 orange.
1 Tumbler of orange
  squash.
$1\frac{1}{2}$ pints of cold water.
Sprigs of mint.
Cucumber peel.
1 tablespoon of sugar.

Put the tumbler of orange squash in a large jug with the one and a half pints of water. Squeeze the juice from half the orange and add to this. Cut the other half into thin slices and float on top.

Stir in a tablespoon of sugar making sure it dissolves and drop in a few sprigs of mint. Cut a few long strips of peel from a cucumber and slide down the side of the jug. Cool thoroughly before drinking. The cucumber and mint give it an added flavour.

You can of course use lemon squash and a lemon if you prefer, or grapefruit. Another way is to mix them; use half of each squash and either half each of the orange or lemon, or use both and add some more water.

A few lumps of ice dropped in make it a much more refreshing drink on a hot day. A good cooling mixture to use in the absence of a refrigerator is a handful of washing soda and a handful of cooking salt in a little water. Stand the jug in this for a while.

HERB TEAS

Many folk grow herbs in their gardens, especially the commoner ones such as mint, sage, thyme and marjoram. These, if made into tea, all have some special medicinal property, known for hundreds of years by the gypsies and country folk.

Some leaves and flowers of other plants are also used in this way; most are made by pouring hot water on the fresh or dried leaves and leaving the brew to stand for a few minutes in the same way as ordinary tea.

Some of the herbs, such as sage and thyme are evergreen, but I always dry some. The most usual way of drying herbs is to hang them in bunches in a warm room and leave them to dry. I think they get dusty this way, so I wash mine and dab the leaves dry with a cloth, then spread them out on tins and dry slowly in an oven, at the lowest setting. It takes hours, and one must be careful not to over-dry them. Leave the oven door open slightly to let the moisture escape quickly. When they are dry the leaves can easily be stripped from the stalks and stored in screw top jars.

BLACKCURRANT TEA

This is very good for colds, and as a preventative or relief for sore throats.

If the blackcurrants are in season, boil those and use the juice with some sugar added. But colds are not so prevalent when blackcurrants are ripe; I expect if you have blackcurrants in the garden you make jam from them, or if not you could buy a good brand from the shop. A tablespoon of this jam in a glass of hot water is a quick way to make a soothing drink. To make it more nourishing for an invalid, add the jam to a glass of hot milk.

COLTSFOOT TEA

This is very good for coughs; I can recommend this as we have often taken it.

Gather a few leaves of coltsfoot; they are big and thick, rather like an overgrown primrose leaf; so you will not need many. Put them in a saucepan with a pint of water and simmer for twenty minutes. Add the juice of a lemon and some strips of peel, and simmer for another five minutes. Strain the liquid off and sweeten to taste with honey or brown sugar. It can be kept for a few days, but as I have said before, it will turn into wine if it is kept too long.

CARAWAY SEED TEA

These can be grown in the garden. The plants look very much like carrots while growing. The seeds are good for flatulency, and from the taste of caraway seed tea, I should imagine that gripe water for babies is made from the same thing. With a little sugar added, the tea is quite a pleasant drink. I like it, but then I always did pinch the baby's gripe water!

Crush the seeds, or buy the already rolled ones; you will need half an ounce to half a pint of water. Put the seeds in a jug and pour on half a pint of boiling water, stir well, then cover the jug and leave to stand overnight. I usually add some sugar when the mixture is hot. Strain the liquid off and bottle it. Put the cork in tight. Do not keep it for more than a week or so. It is best to make a small amount and have it fresh. A spoonful of this will relieve the 'wind'.

CARROT TEA

This is supposed to relieve gout, I don't suffer from it — not yet, anyway, so cannot vouch for the cure, but I have been told that it is good.

Scrub a large carrot and slice it thinly into a saucepan, and add half a pint of water. Put the lid on and boil for forty minutes. Strain off the carrot liquid and drink a cup of this night and morning.

I expect the treatment would have to be continued for some time to have any effect.

CAMOMILE FLOWERS TEA

These are for clearing the blood and to relieve headaches. The dried flowers can be bought from the chemist.

Put a pinch of the flowers in a cup and pour on boiling water. Cover the cup and leave it for about five minutes, then drink it while still hot.

CELERY TEA

This is good for rheumatism, they say, either the stalk or the seed can be used.

Boil a few stalks of celery or ½ oz. of seed in a pint of water for about half an hour, then strain the liquid off and take a glass every day.

I believe eating raw celery is meant to be equally beneficial, but some people find this hard to digest.

CLOVE TEA

This is also good for flatulency.

Put four or five cloves in a small cup and pour on boiling water. Crush the cloves a little, then cover the cup and leave for five minutes. Sip it while it is hot.

HOP TEA

Hops seem to be a cure for numerous complaints. They act as a tonic, a cure for indigestion; to regain a lost appetite and many other things. No wonder beer is so popular! Taken hot, hop tea is a cure for sleeplessness.

Put a handful of hops in a jug and pour on a pint of boiling water. Cover the jug and leave until cold. Take a small glassful when necessary.

MARJORAM TEA

This is said to relieve headaches.

Put a teaspoon of marjoram leaves, fresh or dried in a teacup and pour on boiling water. Cover the cup with a saucer and leave for about five minutes, then sip it while hot.

MINT TEA

This is also good for headaches and helps to relieve flatulence. I think it is quite pleasant to drink.

Put a few leaves, dried or fresh, into a cup and pour on boiling water. Cover the cup and leave for a few minutes. Sip it while hot. For flatulence, add a pinch of bicarbonate of soda.

SAGE TEA

This can be used as a gargle or as a hairwash; it is supposed to darken the hair and prevent greyness.

To make it, you need a handful of fresh or dried sage leaves, placed in a jug and a pint of boiling water poured over. Stir well, then cover the jug and leave it to get cold. Strain, and use as a gargle or hairwash.

THYME TEA

This is a very good relief for whooping cough. A little taken when the cough is troublesome is said to bring speedy relief. It can also be used as a gargle for sore throats.

Put a small teaspoonful of fresh or dried thyme leaves in a cup and pour on boiling water. Cover the cup and leave it for a few minutes to infuse, then sip it while hot, or cool it for a gargle.

DANDELION COFFEE

This is not a herb tea, but as it is a drink, I thought I would include it. I have been told that dandelion roots make very good coffee, very much like the real thing. It is quite simple to make. Scrub the root, then bake it in a slow oven until it is quite dry. Grate it very finely, then use in the same way as coffee. I always mean to try it, but when I think of it I never seem to have a fork handy to dig the root. If the price of coffee goes up any more, I certainly shall give it a try.

INDEX